T0087598

THE REGENSBURG LECTURE

"The greatest events and thoughts – but the greatest thoughts are the greatest events – are comprehended last: the generations which are their contemporaries do not *experience* such events – they live past them."

– Nietzsche, *Beyond Good and Evil*, #285

Other Titles of Interest from St. Augustine's Press

James V. Schall, S.J., *The Sum Total of Human Happiness*

James V. Schall, S.J., *The Modern Age*

Thomas Aquinas, *Commentary on Aristotle's Nicomachean Ethics*

Thomas Aquinas, *Commentary on Aristotle's De Anima*

Thomas Aquinas, *Commentary on Aristotle's Metaphysics*

Thomas Aquinas, *Commentary on Aristotle's On Interpretation*

Thomas Aquinas, *Commentary on Aristotle's Posterior Analytics*

Thomas Aquinas, *Commentary on Aristotle's Physics*

Thomas Aquinas, *Disputed Questions on Virtue.*

Thomas Aquinas, *Commentary on the Epistle to the Hebrews*

Thomas Aquinas, *Commentary on St. Paul's Epistles to Timothy, Titus, and Philemon*

John of St. Thomas, *Introduction to the Summa Theologiae of Thomas Aquinas.* Translated by Ralph McInerny

St. Augustine, *On Order [De Ordine]*

Karel Wojtyła (John Paul II) *Man in the Field of Responsibility*

Josef Pieper, *Scholasticism: Personalities and Problems*

Josef Pieper, *The Silence of St. Thomas*

Josef Pieper, *In Tune with the World: A Theory of Festivity*

C.S. Lewis and Don Giovanni Calabria, *The Latin Letters of C.S. Lewis*

Rémi Brague, *Eccentric Culture: A Theory of Western Civilization*

Rémi Brague, *On the God of the Christians*

Joseph Owens, C.Ss.R, *Aristotle's Gradations of Being in Metaphysics E-Z*

Leo Strauss, *Xenophon's Socrates*

Leo Strauss, *Xenophon's Socratic Discourse: An Interpretation of the Oeconomicus*

Ralph McInerny, *The Defamation of Pius XII*

Bernard J. O'Connor, *Papal Diplomacy: John Paul II and the Culture of Peace*

Bainard Cowan, ed., *Gained Horizons: Regensburg and the Enlargement of Reason*

THE REGENSBURG LECTURE

James V. Schall, S.J.

ST. AUGUSTINE'S PRESS
South Bend, Indiana

Manufactured in the United States of America.

2 3 4 5 6 7   19 18 17 16 15 14 13

Library of Congress Cataloging in Publication Data
Schall, James V.
The Regensburg lecture / James V. Schall.
p. cm.
Includes bibliographical references and index.
ISBN 1-58731-695-1 (hardcover: alk. paper)
1. Benedict XVI, Pope, 1927- Glaube, Vernunft und Universität.
2. Faith and reason – Christianity. 3. Catholic Church –Doctrines.
I. Benedict XVI, Pope, 1927– Glaube, Vernunft und Universität.
English. II. Title.
BT50.B363S53 2007
230'.2 – dc22   2007000834

St. Augustine's Press
www.staugustine.net

TABLE OF CONTENTS

ACKNOWLEDGMENTS

This book arose from two essays originally published on-line by Ignatius Insight, 1) "The Regensburg Lecture," September 15, 2006 and 2) "Ratzinger at Regensburg: On What Is a University?" September 18, 2006. Also related was my interview on the lecture published on Zenit, October 3, 2006. Bruce Fingerhut, Director of St. Augustine's Press, kindly suggested these reflections be expanded into the present book. The first appendix is the text of the Regensburg Lecture itself. Its paragraphs follow those of the text in *L'Osservatore Romano*, English, September 20, 2006, but I have added the numbers of paragraphs. The second appendix had been published on-line at Ignatius Insight on August 15, 2006 and republished here with permission of Ignatius Insight.

INTRODUCTION

I.

Benedict XVI has written in German some seventy books and hundreds of essays. Much of his work has been or is being translated into English and other languages. While he was for twenty years with the Vatican Congregation, he continued his own theological and philosophical reflections in interviews, lectures, and other writing. He did this independent scholarship because he understood that it was important to distinguish between what a theological scholar does and what an official in charge of the doctrine of faith does. The two approaches or offices are obviously not contradictory or he could not honestly pursue both. He is not a Latin Averröist who might, in his soul, find the truth of one office to contradict that of the other vocation but still decide to go ahead anyway proclaiming both parts of the contradictory as true. The Catholic soul is not a divided soul. What is characteristically Catholic is the mind that pays full attention to truths of reason and revelation on the basis of the truth that they both belong to a coherent whole.

But what is said as a scholar has a different claim for our attention than what one does in deciding the relation of the deposit of faith to some actual text or issue at controversy. Nor is authority as such irrational. It is reasonable to follow authority provided ultimately authority is based on the testimony of someone who actually witnesses or sees the facts or understands the truth. The intellectual status of the philosopher and theologian is rather that of spelling out and grounding reasons and arguments for or against a given statement of truth. Both are engaged in an enterprise that usually began before their lifetime and will probably extend after their lives are completed. To participate in this on-going enterprise over time is the glory of the human mind. It includes both the knowing of what is true and what is not true and, as much as possible, the reasons why each might be proposed.

After becoming Pope in 2005, Benedict XVI has given hundreds of talks of varying length and for differing purposes. He has written one encyclical, *Deus Caritas Est*, to which he often refers in his later addresses and writings. No doubt, even though he is not quite as productive in daily output as his beloved predecessor, John Paul II, Benedict remains prolific. No academic can look at his *opera omnia* without a touch of astonishment at its breadth and depth. One might even surmise that perhaps this man is Pope precisely to call our attention to the profundity and clarity of what he has to tell us. This is something we might overlook were he to remain a mere theologian, philosopher, or curial official. The "wholeness" of truth is, indeed, an abiding theme in the works of Benedict as it is in the work of any serious philosopher. He speaks of theology as a "necessary part of the 'whole' of the *universitas scientiarum*" (#5).

The "wholeness" of all things to be known, something that fascinated a Plato, an Aristotle, an Aquinas, a Dante, cannot leave anything out and still claim to be concerned with the full scope of mind. The whole of *what is* constitutes and includes the truth of *what is*. Philosophy is the quest for knowledge of the whole, a quest that, in principle, cannot omit any claim to the truth of things and still claim to be open to all things. This same quest, as we learn from Augustine, also seems to be at the bottom of that dynamism that charges our souls as we seek to know *what is*.

To come to a fair assessment of Joseph Ratzinger will take time and a profound knowledge of all his works and the subsequent deeds of his Pontificate as they unfold. We recall the famous Persian passage that Aristotle cited, namely, "call no man happy until he is dead." We can expect and anticipate more insight will come from any man who is still alive. But we understand mortality, including the mortality of popes and of our kind. Such mortality is itself included in understanding the human condition. The present small study thus is not intended to be a retrospective overview or critique of all of Benedict's work. Though violent threats have indeed been heard against him, against his life, he remains very much alive and occupied with his office, an office of tremendous scope. Like Christ Himself, popes teach by words and deeds. Words are carefully chosen to point to the truth, to the reality from which they arise. Deeds often speak louder than words, something we recall from the events surrounding the assassination attempt against John Paul II in St. Peter's Square.

While I have been steadily reading him for many years, I realize that much is yet to be learned from what Pope Benedict has already written. Like all profound thinkers, he is a man who frequently needs to be read and reread. I have found him to possess the clearest of minds. Some find him more "Augustinian" than "Thomist," but, even if I found that some sort of problem, I am reminded that Aquinas constantly cited Augustine. In any case, this small book claims no private knowledge or esoteric profundity. It is the reflection of an academic observer on what was presented in an academic forum in which a remarkably concise statement of the meaning of our times was presented for serious reflection. The audience was composed of free and intelligent men and women concerned, as best they can, with the truth of things.

I am aware that opposition to the very statement of truth, even to its possibility, frequently arises from misunderstanding or ignorance. These are sources, however, that can usually be worked out by the normal intellectual endeavors of clarification and understanding. Neither of these latter, misunderstanding and ignorance, is necessarily rooted in problems of contrary will and or other choices about how we ought to live. Often opposition to truth, however, rises from the unsettling suspicion that the truth might well be true, that it might in fact oblige us to live in ways other than in the ways in which we do live. To reject truth, as we are always free to do, also has an intellectual root. This counter-explanation has to be formulated in divergent positions and arguments that serve to justify one's own contrary position.

For not a few, it would be a distinctly unsettling thing if, in the end, the Pope of Rome proved indeed to be a man of superior intelligence who did understand the truth of things and the nature of modernity, with its science and its intellectual foundations. Even worse would it be if it was a pope who states most succinctly and accurately the modern mind's relation to revelation as itself an intelligible enterprise. Put more positively, however, we really want to hear a clear, insightful statement of our condition. If it is a pope who can best present the dimensions of what we need to know, we are less than human if, on such a ground, we refuse to consider it.

II.

This being said, Benedict XVI has an amazing capacity to get to the heart of things. He is a wise man in the proper sense of that term. That is, he knows how to find the order in things. He knows the foundational issues. He knows our proper end and the means to attain it. He knows that he did not invent philosophy or revelation. He is rather entrusted with the task of keeping them as they were handed on to him so that, through them, we may understand what is at issue. He is like a master builder who, on seeing what havoc has happened to a construction because of a storm, nevertheless knows how to repair it, how to put things back in their proper sequence. He is able carefully to distinguish things, the crucial and central task of the genuine philosopher.

Benedict is obviously learned in the academic sense of that term. He is degreed and experienced in things of the mind and the workings of academies. He possesses that thorough erudition typical of rigorous German scholars trained in good German universities. But he is not a pedant or a Gnostic whose understanding, even if it requires considerable effort and genius to learn and expound it, is meant for only a few. He understands that both revelation and philosophy, in their essential truths, are intended for everyone, both as norms in what to know and guides about how to live a reasonable life on the basis of what we know. An occasion to speak to academics in a university setting does not imply that the same knowledge is not also intended in an indirect fashion for everyone else after their own manner of receiving it. The truth, including the truth of revelation, is, ultimately, free, both on the side of God and on the side of man. But we are not free to make up what it is. We are rather free to know and accept it for what it is, to understand why it is so. This understanding is what ultimately makes us free.

Since the election of Leo XIII in 1878, we have only had ten popes. Aside from John Paul I, most of them have reigned for a fairly long time. Leo and John Paul II each occupied the papal office for a quarter of a century. All modern popes have been intelligent men, some of major intellectual powers, none more so that Pope Ratzinger. If we recall, Thomas Aquinas, perhaps the greatest mind of them all, was not a pope, nor was Augustine, nor Newman. Scholars, for the most part, best not be popes or princes, for that matter, though occasionally they work out fine. Being excellent in study is not necessarily the prime qualification for being excellent in the capacity to rule well. But it does not hurt either. Though not a few have so been, popes need not themselves be professors or scholars. But when they are, though it may cause some confusion, it can be a good thing for the Church and the world. Light and illumination about the human condition and its destiny are always welcome when our souls are ready to receive them.

Chances are, however, that a professorial pope will demand of his listeners a high level of careful reading and intelligent reflection to understand what he is about. He will be much more demanding on intellectuals, that usually proud and often touchy lot, than on ordinary people. The former, the scholars, cannot so easily avoid the implications of his arguments if the pope's intellectual stature stands on the same natural grounds as theirs. Yet, as Aquinas showed, intelligence is not intended to obscure but clarify things, even for beginners and for those who have no intention of being philosophers. Well-ordered minds are their own delights.

Moreover, intelligence is not intended merely to pose questions about fundamental issues, but to provide answers that must be reckoned with. In one sense, questions are only seen as questions in their full dimensions when we know the answers to them, including answers that are erroneous answers. This "answer-oriented" aspect is one of the most noticeable things that revelation adds to the questions that philosophers ask, or should ask. We begin to suspect that revelation must be taken seriously when we realize that our genuine and highest philosophical questions are better answered by revelation than by philosophy itself, but, nonetheless, not contrary to philosophy.

III.

What interests me here is the lecture that Benedict XVI gave at the University of Regensburg on September 12, 2006, during his apostolic visit to his homeland in Bavaria. When I first read this lecture, a day or so after it was given, but before the Muslim world was aware of it, I was immediately struck both by its brevity and by its brilliance, two qualities, when taken together, I find compelling. Far from being just another papal or academic address, this lecture clearly went to the heart of things that count. It riveted my attention on the whole scope of our history and our intelligence.[1] When I first read this lecture, the text of which appears in the appendix to this book, I knew something

---

1   The Regensburg Lecture, as I told a class at the time, reminded me in scope of two other essays: (1) Hans Urs von Balthasar, "A Résumé of My Thoughts," *Communio*, 15 (Winter, 1988) [www.ignatiusinsight.com/features2005/print2005/hub_resume_print.html] and (2) Robert Sokolowski, "Phenomenology and the Eucharist," *Christian Faith & Human Understanding* (Washington: The Catholic University of America Press, 2006), 69–85.

momentous had happened in the human mind. Something was said here that no one else had been saying. Sorting out what was spoken in Regensburg is, I think, an intellectual enterprise that awaits the attention of every person who is concerned about intelligence and truth and, indirectly, about their consequences in the realm of action. This lecture is one of the fundamental tractates of our time. It is almost the first one that really understands the fuller dimensions of what our time is intellectually about.

The reaction in the Arab world a couple of days after this lecture, in which the Holy Father cited a passage unflattering of Mohammed, has made it, to many, infamous or foolhardy. He should not, we are told, have said what he said. He was "undiplomatic," "insensitive," even that cardinal sin, "un-ecumenical." To others, however, it was a lecture of profound insight that requires much attention, not merely, or even mainly, because of what it said about Islam but because of what it said about our world, about our own souls, and through them about the condition of the world as a whole. The lecture itself was something that enlightens our minds about the whole of our reality.[2] It is one of those formulations of mind in search of truth that we must reckon with. It helps us to reflect on *everything that is*. It makes us realize that a whole age may not understand what it is about in its own soul.

In the months after the lecture was first given, an almost infinite number of comments, analyses, recriminations, enco-

2 See what Benedict XVI says of his use of these texts in the footnotes to the text of the Regensburg Lecture, below, pp. 147-48.

mia, and reactions have been printed throughout the world. No doubt the best of these will be collected in a volume or two shortly. I do not conceive my purpose here to survey these reactions, though I have read a number of them, both favorable and unfavorable to what the Pope said. Rather here I want to present a sustained argument about the lecture's overall significance. It was an argument that existed first of all, in true Aristotelian fashion, "for its own sake." It intended to state a truth. It claims no other authority but its argument for it. Here Benedict does not say "believe what I say," or "this teaching is or is not in conformity with classical revelational teaching." Rather he says, "this is the argument as I understand it." His first task as a lecturer and our first task as readers are in the realm of intellect, of understanding what is said.

In the case of this kind of a lecture, then, we are not asked to "believe" the Pope in some theologically technical sense of that noble word. We are rather asked to grasp his argument. The lecture now exists as something we are free to consider and apprehend, but only if we choose to do so. We can refuse to think about it. We can, if we have grounds, reject it. What it said, however, went to the very heart of our minds and souls. It did something that could not be done in politics, which is primarily taken up with actions and passions and presupposes, though it does not always possess a prior clarity of thought sufficient to guide action. What the Pope did was nothing less than straighten out our minds about where we are and what we are about. Acting correctly presupposes thinking correctly, presupposes understanding *what is.*

Moreover, it is a difficult thing to understand, state, and accept the truth, however much these efforts constitute the real purpose of our minds. We can see both in our revelational and in our philosophic traditions that truth is not always or even often accepted and kept. But truth is never rejected without proposing a counter-theory or proof that would justify this rejection. That is, we ironically cannot be "unreasonable" without, at the same time, being reasonable, without giving reasons for our deviations from reason. Such counter-theories, in the form of ideologies or myths, become themselves aspects of understanding the whole truth about something. To understand truth, it is necessary to understand the plausible errors surrounding it and arguments against it.

Benedict himself touched on this issue when, near the end of his lecture, something to which I shall return later in these reflections, he cited, wisely, the very founder of philosophy, Socrates himself. "Here I am reminded of something Socrates said to Phaedo. In their earlier conversations, many false philosophical opinions had been raised, and so Socrates says, 'It would be easily understandable if someone became so annoyed at all these false notions that for the rest of his life he despised and mocked all talk about being – but in this way he would be deprived of the truth of existence and would suffer a great loss" (#61, 90c–d). To be "deprived of the truth of existence" because of annoyance at false issues is indeed the greatest of losses.

It should not pass without notice that in the passage in the *Phaedo* immediately before that cited by Benedict, we read:

You know how those in particular who spend their
time studying contradiction in the end believe
themselves to have become very wise and that they
alone have understood that there is no soundness or
reliability in any object or in any argument, but that
all that exists simply fluctuates up and down as if it
were in the Euripus [violent Greek sea straits] and
does not remain in the same place for any time at all
(90b–c).

Already here we have the dimensions of modern relativism
that Benedict sees as basic to the intellectual disorders of
our public life. The voluntarism that he sees in many
strands of Islamic theology has, in principle, the exact same
effect. In neither system can we find "any soundness or reliability in any object or in any argument" because everything *that is* can, on such philosophic principle, be otherwise.

Indeed, we live in a culture, as Benedict has frequently
remarked, that denies that truth is either desirable or possible or anything but relative. Of course, relativism is itself
a theory that is either true or false, one that also can be
examined for its validity by the mind. Its own inner coherence has itself long been examined in our tradition of reasoned discourse. Relativism claims as a truth the truth that
truth is not stable over time or across space. No one, however, can really "think" this position. The very formulation
of relativism as true involves a contradiction of its premises that we have no truth.

The examination of philosophic and theological theses

is no mere sidelight or academic game, nowhere less so than in the papacy or indeed in contemporary politics. Kingdoms and peoples rise and fall on account of which principles, of which understanding of truth or its lack, they or their enemies accept and act. The first lines of battle, and of peace, are in the mind and heart. It is into this "strait," to recall Plato, which the Pope's lecture rightly proposes to plunge. It is, in context, a brave and even personally dangerous endeavor.

When one undertakes to write a short book on a lecture that itself had fewer than 4,000 words in its original delivery, some lack of proportion may seem evident. Why say more when what was said was so spare, so precise? The brevity of the Pope's lecture was part of its genius, part of why it is memorable. It is more difficult to say fundamental things in a short space than to speak or write of them in long tomes. One might think, and justly, that it is better just to read the original lecture. And of course, this lecture must be read and reread. There is no substitute for reading it. While it is a formal, academic lecture, that, as I shall explain in the first chapter, has its own purpose and spirit, it is fundamentally intelligible to a normal reader in its general import. Most people, as Chesterton might say, are not learned but they are not idiots; they have common sense. They too seek to know and expect clarity from those of more leisure and genius than they.

IV.

When one thinks of great historical addresses and essays,

such as Cicero's *Pro Archia*, Pericles' Funeral Oration, Plato's *Apology*, Paul's Epistle to the Ephesians, Henry V's Speech on St. Crispin's Day, Lincoln's Gettysburg Address, Dostoyevsky's Address at the Unveiling of the Monument to Pushkin, Solzhenitsyn's Harvard Lecture, or some of Churchill's war-time addresses, we realize that what moves the world does not have to be, indeed should not be, long or complicated. Ultimate things can be briefly stated and are, as Plato intimated in the *Gorgias*, better said that way. In fact, as we learn from Aquinas, a statement of ultimate things needs to be relatively concise, profound, to the point. As an event, Pope Ratzinger's lecture at Regensburg, in its long-range importance, can only be compared with John Paul II's first visit to Poland. Events need not be words. But words can also be events. Words at their best are intended to move us. And they do move us. But academic words have a somewhat different purpose. They are intended primarily to enlighten us, to take our minds to the heart of *what is*. This enlightenment is the purpose of the Regensburg Lecture. It is what has been lacking in our understanding of where we are.

This lecture begins, as I shall indicate further in speaking of suicide bombings, with the most obvious perplexity in contemporary world society, namely "is the use of violence permitted to expand religion?" Not only is it permitted but are those who practice this violence on themselves or others, by their very violence, practicing reason and virtue? We used to ask this first question of communist thinking, though that was related to ideology, not to religion. Koestler's novel *Darkness at Noon* is about the Rousseauian "self-confession" of members of the Communist Party who had fallen out of favor. They "confess" and are immediately executed. This horror is perhaps as close as modern ideology ever came to the implications of the acts of contemporary suicide bombers. These latter, following a certain line of theology, see themselves as performing redemptive acts. These acts, in causing the violent deaths of oneself and others, enable their perpetrators to reach Paradise because of them. Simultaneously, they are designed to further the cause of Islam in the world.

This query thus leads us to existing theories that not only hold but often insist that violence is related to religion. On what, if any, intellectual basis might such a position be maintained? Is it merely preposterous, as the "terrorist" name we give to it seems to presuppose, at least in our minds? Is it simply unthinkable? This reasoning is what we want to understand. Can such a view be "reasonable?" To think about this issue as presented is not an insult to religion or to anyone who might hold such a view. Rather, it is a necessary factor in reason's own self-understanding. To respond to such a wonderment about which many, besides himself, are concerned, the Pope needs to explain the history and intelligibility of what is the meaning of "what it means to be reasonable."

Benedict argues that a tradition from the Greek philosophers maintains that such use of violence is, in principle, "unreasonable." He does not think this conclusion of unreasonableness to be only "Greek," even though Greek thinkers were leaders in its formulation. It is reflective of the structure of mind and reality. He thus must explain the relation of this tradition of reason to revelation in the Jewish, Christian, and Muslim senses. The issue already existed outside of Jewish and Christian revelation in the fertile mind of the classic Greek thinkers, who also understood, simultaneously, the attractiveness of relativism. Not a lot is new under the sun.

Following this explanation, the Pope indicates why this position that "violence is reasonable" is precarious. Already in the late Middle Ages among Christians, however, some principles were formulated that seemed to justify it. Modern philosophy is seen in this lecture as a steady and gradual effort to eliminate any understanding of reason that would prevent man from doing whatever he wills. Hence modernity is seen as an effort to "dehellenize," that is, to get rid of Greek thought and principles. This effort entails a discussion of the meaning of reason in modern science and whether it is the only or prime understanding of reason. What Benedict finally suggests is that any kind of reason must be protected from a concept of voluntarism that would justify violence in the name of reason or God. Thus, this whole lecture is based upon a sustained argument about reason.

The first order of business, paradoxically, is whether it is reasonable to speak of reason in universities. Or better stated, "why do institutions exist that are specifically set aside so that we can first freely articulate the problem as a problem without fear of personal, political, religious, or institutional retaliation?" Obviously, the history of Christianity also suggests that this freedom does not in practice automatically exist. In history, it is rare that regimes exist in which such questions are freely discussed. But even in the worst regimes, we still must seek, stand for, and state the truth. Even though violent death takes place in both cases, martyrdom, the being killed for belief and truth, is radically different from suicide bombing, the positive killing of oneself and others. This difference too is what the Regensburg Lecture was about.

Ever since Christ's third temptation in the desert, that is, his being offered the whole world if, falling down, He would adore the devil, it is possible to envision the whole world worshipping God in a false way, that is, in a way that was not intended in revelation. Revelation was designed to teach the proper way to worship God, something the philosophers had long wondered about. The problem with Marxism was that it confused the Second Great Commandment of "loving thy neighbor" with the First Commandment, with loving God first. The present problem is more with the First Commandment itself, not with "*an sit Deus?*" but with "*quid sit Deus?*" The question of the truth of the revelations, or perhaps better the question of which revelation is true, thus, cannot be avoided. This latter question is why, in the Regensburg Lecture, the question of Greek philosophy is posed also as an element of the faith, properly distinguished and understood.

Chapter I.

A UNIVERSITY LECTURE

"It is a moving experience for me to be back in the university and to be able once again to give a lecture from this podium" (#2).

"To rediscover it [reason] constantly is the great task of the university" (#63).

I.

Both the first and last full paragraphs of Benedict XVI's Regensburg Lecture contain the word, "university." The memorable final sentence tells us that the constant task of the university is to "rediscover *logos*," that is, reason. This urging to *re-discover* implies that we have once discovered it. Perhaps we have neglected it, or lost it, or even deliberately rejected it. It also implies that we can recognize reason when we confront it. We have the inner structure of our being designed to do so. We have a capacity to be reasonable. We are indeed, as Aristotle taught us, "rational animals." This union of mind and body is not only our status in being but also the activity that most characterizes us as beings in the world.

This "continued" rediscovery of reason clearly is not a "once only" endeavor, but something to which we must "constantly" attend. The point seems to be that until the university mind is straightened out, political action, perhaps through no direct fault of its own, will be confused or misdirected. This clarification by reason is perhaps the modern form of the spiritual power and the temporal power. Or, better, we must ask: "what is the reason to which revelation is addressed?" Is there not some sense in which reason must exist before revelation can speak to it? Is this the meaning of the "Greek mind" in the Regensburg Lecture? "The encounter between the Biblical message and Greek thought did not happen by chance" (#19). Reason itself must be "reasonable" to grasp what revelation is about. This is why, as it says in *Fides et Ratio*, that revelation must itself be concerned with not just any philosophic thought, but with philosophy itself oriented to *what is*.

The Pope's introductory words at the University of Regensburg are likewise familiar ones to those who have spent their lives in or around universities. The words initially reveal a formal graciousness and a homey affection, a bit of nostalgia even. Before him are friends and colleagues of previous years. He no longer will he, such is his destiny, return among them as an every-day colleague. He will not retire to Bavaria as he had hoped to do before his elevation to the papacy. Officials of the university, students, members of the Bavarian government, of the city of Regensburg, and of the local diocese are there in the Aula Magna of the University of Regensburg. We are mindful of John Paul II at Krakow and Lublin during his visits to universities in Poland. Popes have a personal history that they bear in their very lives. Authority is also visible and can speak. Those chosen to embody it always come from somewhere, a comforting human thought.

Benedict is inevitably bound up with German university life, as was John Paul II bound to the university life of Poland. A man does not set aside this character or background when he becomes pope, nor do we want him to do so. He does not cease to love his homeland, his university, his family. It would be a sad world if John XXIII forgot Italy, or John Paul II forgot Poland, or Benedict XVI forgot Bavaria. Moreover, it is precisely because Benedict is Pope that, at times, a university lecture, by being what it is, can become useful to him. It enables him to accomplish what he needs to do in the pursuit of his office. Of Benedict XVI, we can use the expression, "Professor Pope," not to suggest that this academic background describes all or primarily what he is as pope. But, it does emphasize, should he choose to speak as a professor, that the capacity and qualification to do so are also his by any criterion of academic life itself.

But an academic lecture itself, in principle, even when delivered by a pope, must remain what it is, a reflective, reasoned presentation of the truth as understood and formulated by a free man. It is given before an audience prepared and willing peacefully to listen to and consider this argument as presented. Benedict understood, I think, that to state what must be said in the historic moment in which he lived, he had to speak, on certain issues, this one in particular, academically. He had simply to state, accurately, and forcefully, the issue at hand. This contemplative purpose is not Lenin's famous activist question, "what is to be done?" Understanding was Benedict's prime and most pressing purpose. No one else, especially in the academy itself, was really making this essential clarification of mind about our present lot. The public order was perplexed because the intellectual order was confused. Not knowing is always precarious.

This statement of what was at issue, with its intrinsic intelligibility, was what was not being presented in the public order. Part of the reason it was not articulated, aside from real fear of retaliation, was an intellectual failure or moral refusal to understand our intellectual and revelational history as, over time, it impinged on our world. At Benedict's election to the papacy, it was frequently said that a German pope might be what is most needed to save Europe, a continent seen in rapid demographic and moral decline, but itself the heart of Christendom. It is not without interest that the question of "what is Europe?" forms a central theme of this lecture. St. Benedict (d. 547), to recall, has long been the patron saint of precisely Europe.

Clearly, although many famous lectures have been given in German universities over the past centuries, an ordinary professorial lecture presented at a contemporary German, or any other, university, however excellent, does not capture anywhere near the publicity that is accorded to one given by a pope on a state visit. A pope is scrutinized even by how he greets his staff in the morning or by what he has for supper or by what he says to little children. This Regensburg Lecture, moreover, as we noted, might have also passed relatively unnoticed, as did many of John Paul II's important university lectures, had this particular lecture not contained, as a necessary part of its argument, something considered more newsworthy and polemical. Had no Muslim reaction occurred, very few would have taken this lecture with the seriousness that it deserves and, more importantly, with the seriousness that the Pope intended for it. If the Pope had cunningly devised a shrewd way to call international attention to his argument, he could not have done anything better than what he did in citing the medieval Persian gentleman on the theoretical question of what Islam holds.

Muslim reaction in fact made the lecture a political phenomenon and intellectual issue that everyone must reckon with. It dealt with an issue everyone must deal with, whether he likes it or not. Ironically, the best way for the Muslim world to have prevented intellectual attention to itself, because of the religious violence evidently coming from many sources identifying themselves as Muslim, would have been to ignore the address. The extent and nature of the reaction as it quickly spread throughout the Muslim world made this reaction seem rather programmed, almost an admission that Islam did not want the issue talked about in any forum. Whether the Pope anticipated this reaction would happen is debated. I suspect, in a general way, that he was not surprised that it did. Precisely this hasty and even violent response is part of what most needs to be discussed, in all its dimensions, beginning in universities.

What the Pope said that is purported to have caused the reaction was integral to the intelligibility of his presentation. To have left it out would have restricted the very purpose for which a lecture is given. Unless the issue is stated as sharply as possible, its central purpose will not be understood. The Pope chose the approach he did, through recalling a medieval Byzantine Emperor in the fourteenth century, to make us aware that this very issue is not so new. The same questions have been constantly arising ever since Muslim armies began to march north, west, east, and south beginning in the eighth century. I would even say that the failure to confront the intellectual and religious roots of this issue in Islam, in the academy, in the Church, and in the state, is one of the main reasons that the problem still exists and continues to grow in seemingly an exponential manner even in our own time.

Paradoxically, then, had the Pope removed the citation about Mohammed (#11), as not a few critics have subsequently insisted that he should have done, the whole lecture might have quietly disappeared in spite of its penetrating analysis of Western intellectual culture. A few days after its presentation, this lecture received world-wide attention because of reaction within the Islamic world. Almost no one outside that particular culture, with its own presuppositions, considered what was said as such to be offensive to anyone either in intent or in context. One might say, in retrospect, as we suggested, that this reaction was what made the lecture of historic significance. But this conclusion would be superficial. Not a few have chastised the Pope for including words that "might" offend. Still few people easily see why citing a passage from a medieval text is itself offensive, unless perhaps, by criteria of modern historiography, the citation was quoted incorrectly, which it was not.

II.

The original citation, moreover, from a Byzantine Emperor in 1391, was itself posed as an honest perplexity to a qualified Persian gentleman. This contrast of views is the stuff of intellectual inquiry. Intellectual issues need first to be stated, refined, and understood accurately. Until this work is accomplished, nothing further can proceed with rationality. Furthermore, the concern of the Byzantine Emperor is, in almost the exact same language, the same one most observers of Islam have in mind today. "Is violence justified on the grounds of religious purpose?" To inquire whether the record of Mohammed is one that has brought violence and evil into the world is neither textually nor historically absurd. Unless it can be shown otherwise in a fair discussion, there is every reason to maintain that the influence of Mohammed did bring these things into the world, even though some may call these results good and others bad. No one has to be a medieval Emperor to worry about the same thing in our own time.

The Emperor Manuel asked an honest question to a

Persian gentleman, himself qualified to answer it. The Persian gentleman at the time did not himself seem to think it was wrong to inquire about this topic. He did not draw a knife or take to the streets. In principle, it cannot be said to be an insult to Mohammed to ask what seems obvious to many, whether he advocated these things. But Mohammed himself, as several studies clearly show, did propose war and struggle as an aid to expand Islam. "But naturally the Emperor also knew the instructions, developed later and recorded in the Qur'an, concerning holy war" (#12). The Pope thus indicated that there is textual evidence in the Koran, among other places, for this concern.

The question then becomes, not to wring our hands over this situation, but to understand why Mohammed or at least some of his followers may have thought violence proper in pursuit of their world-encompassing mission. As the Pope indicates, it is asserted that Mohammed did not advocate this violent approach – "There is no compulsion in religion" (#11). In this case, the problem is not with Mohammed but with other historical Muslims who claim that he did so charge his view to enable him to expand their religion with force. This leaves the internal problem in the hands of those Muslims who claim that there is no relation between Islam and violence and those Muslims who say that this is what Mohammed did teach. Christians, Jews, and other non-Muslims cannot be blamed for wondering which position, for the Muslims themselves, is the correct one and who is qualified to decide. It is obviously an honest inquiry to know the truth of the matter.

Thus, if evidence is given that it was true that Mohammed never advocated violence, then the one who asks the question would have objective reason to change his mind about the evidence. That is, the question that must be asked and answered is this: "is it or is it not true that Mohammed or the Koran permits violence in the name of religion?" To make it an insult, blasphemy, or crime even to ask the question is itself a problem with the most serious consequences. Logically, it means the question can never be objectively answered on the basis of reason. One cannot imagine that Mohammed himself would have been insulted by someone wanting to know the foundations and implications of his own teachings.

The Pope is careful to acknowledge the bluntness of this question of the Byzantine Emperor.

> [The Emperor] addresses his interlocutor [the Persian gentleman] with a startling brusqueness, a brusqueness which leaves us astounded on the central question about the relationship between religion and violence in general, saying, "Show me just what Mohammed brought that was new and, there you will find things only evil and inhuman, such as his command to spread by the sword the faith he preached" (#12).

Yet, the exact same question with the same bluntness can often be found daily on the internet or many free newspapers and journals anywhere in the world. The Pope really did not have to go to a medieval Emperor to find this concern expressed with equal gravity and brusqueness.

What seems lacking most of all, in the light of such questions, is an authoritative and detailed answer to the question as asked, not merely violent protests for asking the question. The angered protests over even asking the question about violence made it seem to most people that few in Islam will face the objective purpose of the question asked – that is, does or does not Islam in principle approve violence? The medieval query is a contemporary query. The reaction proves it. The burning question is not whether this result can be attributed to Mohammed by a Byzantine Emperor who lived seven hundred years ago. Many of Mohammed's present-day adherents maintain that they are following him. Many do frankly claim that violence is to be used in fostering their cause. This claim is not something arbitrarily dreamed up by a medieval Emperor, a contemporary pope, or a hostile Western press.

The proper approach to the question, on the part of adherents of Mohammed, is to answer it, not to maintain that its very posing is itself reprehensible. I know of no one who would not be delighted with a firm adherence to the strict application, legal and moral, of the Koranic principle that "There is no compulsion in religion" (#11). The longer the question is not honestly and officially answered, and the politics based on it still continue, the more the suspicion will grow that in fact violence is justified. It is neither unfriendly nor prejudiced to point out this logic. Nor is it irrational to expect a reasonable answer to the question that can itself be responded to with reason.

The question thus arises, "was the reaction in the Islamic world itself indicative of an intellectual and moral problem within that world, one that it is not itself fully willing to face?" Is the reason why such a consideration of the issue cannot take place itself a serious theological and philosophical issue that needs to be spelled out and faced? If so, is not this very spelling-it-out itself a good thing, a service to everyone, including Muslim thinkers and faithful? If the mere statement of a problem is conceived to be blasphemy, is the solution to the problem simply to urge everyone to "respect religion" and thus not talk about the problem in an academic manner? Do we not, in other words, need a place where we can be as frank as the Byzantine Emperor with the Persian gentleman? Why are we moderns more constrained than those medieval gentlemen? Are we less free in academia than the Byzantine Emperor before the siege of his city? Manuel II and the Persian gentleman did not seem ill at ease or at each other's throats for honestly wondering about an issue that everyone was familiar with and in which they were both involved.

The Pope later apologized if the words cited offended anyone. He thus implied that the citation as such, in the reflective context in which it was given, ought not on any objective grounds to have offended anyone. But he did not retract his basic comment. Nor did he withdraw his position that these issues need to be frankly talked about. The reason he brought the issue up in the first place remained pressing, whatever the reaction. This willingness to converse rather than attack or protest is what he means by being men of peace in the pursuit of a resolution for these matters.

The question of whether anyone should be justly offended by what he said, however, is the real issue. And this latter issue has to do with the question of "what is a university lecture?" Some things need to be addressed, whatever the reaction. Indeed, a university is a place where we can present questions whether they "need" to be addressed or not. We can address there issues simply because we want to know the truth about something. Outside reactions should not be what decide whether an issue needs to be discussed. The outside reaction itself rather indicates the need. Sometimes not to speak the truth is itself an act of cowardice, not of prudence. It takes intellectual courage to state the truth. Courage is not only a military virtue.

III.

What, then, is a university lecture? This question presupposes the very idea of a university. The university as we know it grew out of the structure of the medieval Church. It was intended to be, in one very precise sense, a place set apart. Set apart for what? Many differing kinds of institutions can and should exist within a civil society. The army, the business corporation, the art gallery, the sporting societies, each is different yet each is a definable organization designed for specific purposes that cannot be accomplished without a distinct end or purpose or space to carry out what they are. The university is another of these specialized institutions. It is not the Church. It is not the state. It is not the manufacturing plant. It is not any of the other normal organs of any society. In what, then, does it "specialize"?

Basically the university specializes in knowing, in pursuing the central perfection of our nature, with the added implication that it is seeking to know the truth. Thus, its reasons for knowing are likewise given, after the manner of peaceful and intelligent men, for the examination and corroboration of fair-minded listeners. Thus, knowing what is true in itself involves certain conditions, certain standards and principles of discourse and argument. The university is not the only institution interested in the truth, of course. It would be dangerous if it were. Indeed, everyone is interested in what is true, not just popes or university professors, let us hope. Certainly the Church is and must be interested in and devoted to truth. Indeed, what it is to be a human being includes, at bottom, a desire to pursue and know the truth. Universities, as their best, exist because we respect and defend this deepest of human purposes while providing a place for it to flourish.

Yet university professors themselves, among all human beings, as we learn from someone like Augustine, are most likely to be tempted to conceive their own versions of truth to be the only correct ones. More than any other human group, they are tempted to pride, to identifying too hastily their own ideas with *what is*. Thus, the university is a special place, protected in its existence in a legal and political way. It is designed freely to pursue its proper purpose. But I do not wish to imply it cannot be a spiritually dangerous place both for those in it and for those influenced by it. Almost all disorders of private or public life somehow begin in the souls of an educated elite, of the dons, including the clerical dons, perhaps more especially in them. When academic ideas filter down to practice, they are diluted and often received out of context. But their origins are found in some mind, some mind not necessarily of one's own time or place, some mind free to pursue the truth as it wants it to be for its own purpose or free to pursue it as it is.

When Christians speak of the truth, they are wont to recall the famous scripture passage in John that what will make them "free" is the "truth" – "ye shall know the truth and the truth shall make you free." We are thus not free just to be free. Were that the case, were freedom, without further distinction, simply interchangeable with truth, then everyone's truth would be checked only by itself. Unless some objective criterion of truth is available and acknowledged, unless some reality in fact exists, freedom means little. What after all could it mean to maintain that "my truth is itself constituted by my freedom?" In that case, neither truth nor freedom could exist, but only power unchecked by anything outside of itself. In some basic sense, it is this problem of a freedom unbound by anything but itself that is the real theme of the Regensburg Lecture. It is a problem both in the West and in Islam.

The university is a place that is set aside so that things can be examined by reason. Again, every institution and every person are to be ruled by reason. What is different about the university is that it is a place where coherent ideas and arguments can be presented before those who are themselves trained to listen and respond to argument. If one has to fear for his life or his well being, his faith or his family, he will not, without heroic virtue, be free to present his argument. I do not wish here to go into the idea that the university obviously cannot be a forum for just every nutty idea. We have internet and the press for that. There is a place for people to say what they want however outlandish, give or take the limits of slander and obscenity. These limits themselves are based on a sensible understanding of what we usually less than angelic human beings often do.

The whole latter part of Benedict's address, no doubt, is concerned with the fact that modern universities often betray their own purpose by defining reason solely in terms of verifiable scientific method, a definition that, however useful in its own limited area, narrows the scope of mind. This restriction of method results in a definition of reason that excludes the basic human questions of why we exist and what is our destiny, issues that concern every human being and most of the classic religions (#58). These issues do have a place also in the university, which defines itself as a place where we can freely and without fear of personal injury, talk about the whole, the *universitas scientiarum*. The discourse of the Pope is interesting in that it constantly links both word and truth. Speaking is itself essential to the truth.

What the Regensburg Lecture was, then, was precisely a university lecture. It presupposed from Western tradition that a place existed within society wherein serious issues could be brought up and presented for no other immediate reason but to understand what they are. Thus, it could not be a place where certain issues, such as the relation of religion to violence, had to be withheld, lest somewhere, someone might be offended by the very discussion itself. The whole issue of whether such a place should exist or can exist is brought up by this very lecture.

The fact is that this lecture was presented on the assumption that universities can and ought to exist as places where even a pope can present a discourse whose only purpose is to examine the truth and state his reasons for it. This idea means that the author of an academic discourse is aware of and open to other views. They are indeed incorporated into the discourse itself. The Regensburg Lecture, as such, asks nothing more than its argument. Far from being disrespectful either of Islam or of modern thought, it is almost the first time that the ultimate dimensions of both have been taken seriously and seen in their relationship to each other and to reason.

We need to recognize that "freedom," as something that belongs to each individual person who has a mind capable of discerning its dimensions, is not a philosophic position shared by the Islamic notion of freedom. This latter notion of freedom is something belonging first to the community, which is "free" in the highest sense to obey Allah. Whether Allah has any limits on his freedom is part of the question that the Pope and others ask. If obedience to Allah means that it is possible that violence or jihad be used to extend Islam, then clearly the problem is already phrased in totally different terms. If it is "reasonable" to stipulate that obedience to Allah, the locus of freedom, means doing whatever Allah requires, whatever it is, this interpretation of freedom means that obedience in the Muslim sense is not the same as freedom in the classic sense, though it may be, in effect, compatible with philosophic relativism.

What then was the topic of the Regensburg Lecture? It is an error to think this lecture was principally about Islam, though Islam is also included in its main theoretical thrust. The Pope goes to the heart of a question that is of central concern to every non-Muslim who wants to understand recent events. Beginning with 9/11, though now stretching back two or three decades, perhaps centuries, why does what we call "terrorism" recur? No doubt, at least some Muslims have the same concerns, namely, whether or not a theological understanding or argument exists that justifies violence in the name of this religion, with its "jihad" and the suicide bombers. Is or is not such action justified in Muslim theology? If so, why so? If not, why not?

This question is asked almost everywhere as a genuine perplexity in dealing with the Islamic world. It is not something that is only a question of our era. It is not simply a question of Europe or America, but includes Asia and Africa and many of the world's islands. Not a few who identify themselves as Muslim maintain, without apologies, that violence is indeed justified both in the Koran and in Islamic law and tradition. If no one held that it did or if no one acted on its validity, we would have no problem on this score. In fact, if no one held it, we would have no religious violence to talk about. The argument is sometimes heard that all non-Muslims are historically guilty of repressing Muslims. Therefore, they are not innocent, so it is all right to attack them. This position seems at best a rationalization with little foundation in history or theory. Interestingly, this everyone-is-guilty is one of the main points in modern just-war theory in rejecting the indiscriminate use of weapons or bombings.

The reaction to an inquiry about the reasonableness of its own principles in many Islamic political and religious circles seems, to the outsider, at least, to be that "we will not discuss this issue, nor will we allow anyone else to talk about it. We will not even admit it is an issue. In this regard, the intention of the Regensburg Lecture was to insist that, on any grounds of human dignity, the issue had to be faced. Why, we wonder, is this question difficult to answer? The Pope, like everyone else, would be immensely pleased to have a definitive answer, based on texts, authority, and public scholarly and political foundations. It would be simply wonderful if we saw affirmed, in grounded terms, without ambiguity, that Islam does not now, never did, and cannot affirm that Allah approves violence in his cause, that those who hold otherwise will be expelled from the religion. And if this rejection of violence is the case, then the so-called "terrorists" cannot claim, what they do in fact claim, that they are really the authentic followers of Mohammed, whose religion is destined to rule the world. Such violence is fostered by the religion on its own theological grounds. It does not arrive at this position through some Western political theory, and it is both erroneous and unjust to think that it does. But I shall return to this topic, as it is the one that Pope uses to get to the main point of his lecture, which, again, was not only Islam.

This lecture has fewer than 4,000 words. It covers in one way or another almost every central aspect of theology, philosophy, and culture in a precise, clearly articulated intellectual whole. This presentation is, first of all, a "lecture," something prepared and read by a professor or learned scholar. The Pope was given the occasion in a lecture to speak the truth about something that concerns us all, including Muslims themselves. He is as interested in Muslims understanding him, as he is in our understanding them. This is why this is precisely a philosophy lecture. He could have chosen any number of other topics that might interest his attention and that of his immediate German listeners. In any case, either in this forum or another, this topic, one discussed everywhere, had to be addressed by any responsible thinker seeking to understand central issues of our era, central issues of the mind itself. The objective issue is not something that can be simply avoided or ignored by a pope, as it impinges daily on the lives and duties of much of his adherents. But the concern in Regensburg is with the issue about violence and religion as such.

Before any action can take place, understanding must come first. This understanding is where the difficult work initially lies. The lack of a serious effort first to understand the validity Islam's claims about itself has resulted in a political confusion about what to do about the phenomenon. Unless one's theology is straight, one's politics probably will be skewered. The central issue is not about "terrorism," itself a pure abstraction, but about whether Islam, or many of its followers, thinks that it has the right and duty to use terror to further its religious goals. Obviously, some people do think this.

Whether those who advocate violence's legitimacy be heretics, saints, or fools is for the rest of Islam to judge. It will be visible to us how they decide by their own words and actions. But clearly a significant section of their membership, some estimate between 15 and 25 percent of total world Muslim population, have decided that this connection exists. They accept that it is legitimate both in principle and in the Koran to use violence. It is not enough to repeat again and again that Islam is a religion of peace with no further attempt to explain the violence that has so often come from the depths of this faith.

Moreover, this lecture is given by a man, now the pope, who is a former professor at the university at which he once taught. He is doing the university the honor of giving them his insight into the meaning of things. Universities are and

should primarily be "thought," not "action," places. The
Pope is *not* speaking here dogmatically or authoritatively,
other than the authority of reason itself. His principal concern is to present a valid and coherent argument to the
minds of an audience that can, both politically and intellectually, listen freely to what is said. He does not, however, cease to be pope in giving such a lecture. He does not
put on academic garb. He knows he will be read carefully.
Since he is pope, he will be read all over the world. But the
very nature of any "academic" address as such is intended
for minds wherever they are found. Today's internet and
media make any lecture potentially immediately available
anywhere on the planet. But the nature of the lecture is to
make an argument on the basis of reason, no more, no less.
This is its sole justification for being presented in a university format. Such a presentation, as the Pope indicates, is
proper to Christianity's understanding of itself. Reason is
included in the faith and faith does not contradict reason,
but addresses itself to it. When reason is itself violated,
faith will not easily be heard. Indeed, it will not be logically possible to understand what it is about or to spell out
clearly what it holds of itself.

A university, as we have seen, is a particular kind of
place separate from both the Church and the state, from
the work world and from politics, but still within the culture or general society. It is a place where free exchange of
ideas can go on, but only "according to reason." Not everyone is prepared to follow the terms of this cultural agree-

ment about what a university must be if it is to be what it is. Not every culture or polity allows this conception of a university. Indeed, the origins of the university are, besides the Greek experience, in the medieval Church, where universities as we know them first appeared. They attested to the principle free inquiry, clarity of statement, conditions of logic, and comprehension of the whole were included in this enterprise that we call the university.

The Regensburg Lecture follows the classical canons of academic life and dignity. Within this formal setting, discourse has to be free of outside threats of retaliation or incomprehension of what argument and thought are about. No subject can be excluded from consideration but the consideration must be addressed to reason. The speaker, on finishing his lecture, though he may want action to follow, is content that he freely stated a position that could be understood by reasonable human listeners, a position that spoke the truth. Without this initial effort to understand the truth of a thing, political life and the culture that allows it to flourish will not know right order and truth.

What is to be presented and heard, no more, but no less, is a man's understanding of the truth, with his reasons for it. No one at this point is asked to agree or disagree unless persuaded by argument and evidence. But the arguments as such, not agreement or disagreement, are the issue at hand. And the effects of the lecture may take years, decades, even centuries to be fully comprehended. No one in a university, moreover, is free just to "disagree" on a whim. Argument, thought, must be confronted on its own terms. The refusal to do so or the not-to-allow-such-a-sphere-to-exist is, strictly speaking, a totalitarian position.

The common good requires that the civil society, for its own good, allow and protect this area of free reflection and discourse. It is to be free, and permits issues to be discussed in reason, including those arising from revelation. Not all universities, to be sure, allow this freedom. Not all polities allow this of the universities found within their jurisdiction. This is why we cannot avoid taking a stand on the question of what is a university. In the end, the Pope's "university lecture" was as much a lecture about what a university is as it was a lecture about Islam and modern philosophy.

Chapter II.

VIOLENCE AND GOD'S NATURE

"The Emperor [Manuel II], after having expressed himself so forcefully, goes on to explain in detail the reason why spreading the faith through violence is something unreasonable. Violence is incompatible with the nature of God and the nature of the soul. 'God,' he says, 'is not pleased by blood – and not acting reasonably is contrary to God's nature'" (#13).

"[The Emperor] continues: 'Faith is born of the soul, not the body. Whoever would lead someone to faith needs the ability to speak well and to reason properly, without violence and threats. . . . To convince a reasonable soul, one does not need a strong arm, or weapons of any kind, or any other means of threatening a person with death'" (#13).

"In a world where the name of God is sometimes associated with vengeance or even a duty of hatred and violence, this message [of divine love] is both timely and significant." – Benedict XVI, *Deus Caritas Est*, 2005, #1.

I.

The principal critics of the Pope, in the beginning at least, do not even attempt to engage the argument that he saw fit to place before the human mind for consideration about a serious issue – namely, is it, or is it not, permitted and approved to use violence for religious rule and expansion? The claim is made against the Pope that his mere citing of a text is itself a sign of intent to insult. On the surface, such a reaction seems simply absurd. The proposed rational discourse about violence, in the Pope's mind, is to be brief, short. What can be so difficult about answering it? In the Platonic tradition, the issue deserves a short, unambiguous answer. What is not needed are political or diplomatic declarations that Mohammed was somehow offended by attributing to him what many Muslim believers themselves, on the historical record, attribute to him.

The response to an invitation to academic discourse by threats or even violence is itself an admission that there must be some concern that the answer to the question as asked is, in effect, affirmative. "Violence is justified in the name of religion." Not a few Muslims, of course, agree that it is not so justified. They too usually argue their position on the grounds that reasonableness is one of Allah's attributes. Obviously, no quarrel in principle exists here if Muslim thinkers are held to reason every bit as much as everyone else. But even here, the question comes up whether there are philosophic understandings that explain Allah's freedom so that, in logic, such a claim to reason is incoherent.

But why does Benedict choose this particular example from medieval history and philosophy? As we have suggested, it is because it states most succinctly the issue of principle in its most essential and spare philosophic terms. But as formulated about Islam in particular, Benedict uses this approach of citing an historical incident also in order that he can bring up a much more general and basic problem that is not exclusive to Islam, the problem of whether voluntarism is the basis of reality. Still by using this particular instance of a Byzantine Emperor himself being attacked by Islamic forces, the Pope implicitly reminds us that this topic is not a new problem. Islam in the first hundred years of its existence conquered a good deal of Africa, Spain, and Asia by force of arms. Others have thus wondered about the issue even before Manuel II, as we still wonder about it long after him.

Certain intellectual affinities, moreover, exist between Islamic voluntarism and modern relativism and multiculturalism, something the Pope has long been concerned about. Islam itself, if we read its medieval philosophers, is already caught up in philosophic questions that arise from its own claims to explain and understand what it holds about Allah, how Allah is understood. Like medieval Christian and Jewish theology, that began centuries before Islam appeared on the scene, Islam has had to face the question of what to do with Greek philosophy, its charm and its wisdom. It had to articulate its own basic tenets in intelligible terms that could be tested and judged by reason and mind. Aquinas's *Summa contra Gentiles* is largely an examination of answers to perennial problems given by various Arab philosophers as a result of their reading of the Greek thinkers in the light of the Koran.

The citation about Islam is already placed within a philosophical context about the understanding of God. Is He *logos* or not, is He *sola voluntas* or not. We need to grasp the import of such inquiry. The term, *sola voluntas*, implies a Godhead whose power is not in principle limited even by the principle of contradiction, the principle that governs reason. To those who maintain that God is indeed *sola voluntas*, it becomes blasphemy to imply that He could not approve violence if He willed to use it in the pursuit of His purposes. Any such restriction would be seen as a denial of the omnipotence of God. The Pope cites the Cordova Muslim theologian Ibn Hazm to illustrate this point, though he could have cited any number of other similar sources in Muslim philosophy. "Ibn Hazm went so far as to state that God is not bound even by his own word, and that nothing would oblige him to reveal the truth to us. Were it God's will, we would even have to practice idolatry" (#16). Such questions have long been present in the history of philosophy and theology.

Again, if such a view is not held anywhere in Islam, then there is no problem. But this position is one used to justify an obedience to Allah that has no criterion to judge whether what is practiced or demanded is reasonable or not. The logic of this position is that obedience to Allah is absolute even when unreasonable. Revelation is not itself "obliged by God's own truth." This position affirms that

God is not Himself bound by His own truth. It would limit His glory to impose any restrictions, even that of contradiction. The effect of this view is to eliminate any secondary causality which would attribute to non-divine things an inherent order. Thus, in principle anything could be otherwise. What it is has no foundation, no guarantee of its own truthfulness in being. Reality becomes both enormously mysterious and intrinsically arbitrary. The Pope sees this exact same problem in later Western thought, which is no doubt one of the reasons he has brought the issue up in the first place (#25).

Those who do hold that God or Allah is pure will claim themselves to be pious, to be obedient to God. They are holier, in fact, than those who maintain that this divinity is limited by some "reason," particularly human reason. Divine reason cannot be limited except by itself, which, in logic, means it is not limited even by itself. This remark about absolute obedience to a voluntarist God, however, is one reason why I am reluctant to condemn the "terrorists" on the grounds of theories arising out of Western political science. Terrorism may indeed be wrong, in Western political theory. It may be theologically wrong even in Islam for those who hold that Allah wills to be also "reasonable."

But that wrongness is what the Pope recognizes first needs to be established on solid intellectual grounds through conversation and dialogue with those who see the logic of *sola voluntas* as the definition of Allah. Here lies the real root of terrorism. This is the Allah who wills that all the world be submitted to the rites, principles, and law that are set down in the Koran. Such a voluntarist Allah sees no problem with the use of violence in achieving this purpose. Such a god, in the Christian view, cannot be reasonable. Indeed, he cannot be God. This is why Islam, Judaism, and Christianity must decide whether in fact they do worship the same One God *that is*. Certainly, if the voluntarist Allah is the true conception of Allah, then Christians do not worship the same God.

The Pope states the essence of the problem raised in the medieval conversation in this manner: "The decisive statement in this argument against violent conversion is this: not to act in accordance with reason is contrary to God's name" (#14). This view is "self-evident" in Greek philosophy because God does not contradict himself. That is, God cannot, at the same time, command and not command the use of violence without denying that He has an order within the Godhead. "But for Muslim teaching, God is absolutely transcendent. His will is not bound up with any of our categories, even that of rationality" (#14). Again the problem is not with those who do not hold this philosophic position, but with those who do.

What is the spirit in which such a position should be discussed? Even here, the Pope cites Manuel II: "To convince a reasonable soul one does not need a strong arm, or weapons of any kind, or any other means of threatening a person with death" (#13). The Pope could hardly have found a better statement than this one about the spirit needed for a mutual encounter with Islam and its thought on God. In other words, this issue cannot be solved by arms or weapons, even when victorious. The threat of death is simply another way of saying that the affirmation of truth may well imply martyrdom if continuation in life, in a given polity, requires affirmation of a false understanding of what God is. The shadows of Socrates and Christ are already here. No passage in the lecture is more pertinent about the conditions in which this discussion needs to be pursued.

If, however, God is understood to be only power or a will that transcends reason, then reason is subservient to will. In that case, the only proper relation to Allah would be subservient obedience to whatever is willed, whatever it is. Total obedience becomes the highest virtue. One cannot ask, "obedience to what?" "But in Muslim teaching, God is absolutely transcendent. His will is not bound up with any of our categories, even that of rationality" (#14). Again, if given Muslims do not in fact teach or hold this position, no real difference with them on this score can exist. Even here, this agreement does not exempt anyone from eventually examining the grounds on which rationality is accepted.[1]

Once the Holy Father arrives at this point of a more universal voluntarism, he comes to the main business. He

---

1 Jacques Maritain, in his chapter on "The Problem of World Government," in *Man and the State* (Chicago: University of Chicago Press, 1951), 188–216, sought to anticipate this very question by proposing to having everyone agree on the proposition, say, "violence is irrational," but not being politically concerned with the reasoning why a given religion or philosophy might arrive at this prohibition. He acknowledged that, in the theoretic order, however, the issue had to be faced. It is possible to interpret the Regensburg Lecture as an effort to face the grounds of the theoretical issue.

examines the whole structure of mind in the modern world in its origins. He discusses this topic under the sophisticated name of "dehellenization." This characterizes the systematic effort to remove Greek philosophy, that is, reason, from the requirements of mind. Islam is in the news. Jihad is in the news. Suicide bombers are in the news. No one can totally avoid thinking of these issues and why they might come about. Indeed, ironically, suicide bombing and violence, in their seeming irrationality to most of the normal human race, do serve, as did concentration camps and gulags, to emphasize the causes and the intellectual origins of irrationalism wherever it is found. During the Nazi and Communist eras, we were wont to approach this problem through the denial of God's existence or through a Nietzschean proclamation that God was dead. With the claimed relation of terrorism to Islam, we are reluctantly forced to approach it, ironically, through religion.

One explanation for violence is then clearly "religious," at least in the minds of those who employ it. It holds, as we have seen, that Allah could make what is violent to be good, or what is wrong to be right. Or perhaps more basically, the divine will, presupposed to no *logos*, is what makes right and wrong. But any meaningful distinction between right and wrong ceases to exist if Allah can will one to be the other. We should be aware that this problem already existed in Plato. Indeed, it is a perennial philosophical problem that all philosophers have to wrestle with. In the current version, no objective distinction can exist between the right and wrong that Allah cannot change at will. All we have to do is find out whether he willed it or not.

Thus, in this logic, suicide bombers are practicing not violence but virtue. They maintain that they are being obedient to the will of Allah. Will in this understanding becomes blind power, something that will reappear in Western political thought through Marsilius of Padua and Hobbes. Often, absolute power is proposed as a desperate means to provide an alternative to the implication that no order exists in the universe. Power theories, however, merely substitute the human will for the divine will as the origin of order. Without *logos*, no reason remains for finding any distinction between right and wrong. Thus, reason is what is essential to understand why violence is wrong in principle.

The Pope did not invent this voluntarist theory. He is merely citing its existence and intelligibility, the first and necessary step in intelligence. But the very act of citing a passage includes the understanding of what it means. Islam claims to be a revelation subsequent to Judaism and Christianity. It claims to give the final revelation of God that rejects the previous Christian revelation's two basic tenets about God, the Trinity and the Incarnation. These doctrines are understood to be denials that Allah is one or that Allah is transcendent. Within this claim is an understanding of submission to Allah that cannot question whatever Allah might be said to decree. To do so is blasphemy.

At some point, however, it must be asked, even by Muslims, whether it is reasonable that the revelation to

Mohammed that negated the Trinity and Incarnation is itself reasonable. Of course, for the Muslim, the Christian revelation is itself not reasonable. It is a later accretion that Mohammed is sent to correct. Jesus was only a prophet. The truth of these positions is a proper subject of calm philosophical and theological inquiry. It is not blasphemy, neither for the Christian nor for the Muslim to seek as much understanding as possible of what is to be believed.

The Greek Emperor whom the Pope cites anxiously wants to know whether God can approve violence. Obviously, He can, if He is ruled only by will such that nothing in nature or revelation needs be what it is. On this supposition of pure will, we cannot "reason" with Allah, only obey him whatever he says. The Pope's academic question is this: "Is this view tenable?" Even the Pope would admit in logic that it is if Allah is ruled by a will that has no relation to reason. Much, but not all, Muslim philosophy holds precisely this voluntarist view of the Godhead. Muslim custom and polity decrees uphold it with its law and force. No distinction between God and Caesar exists in Muslim states. The very distinction is a product of Greek and Christian thought. Assuming these are obvious and prevalent statements of what is held in that sector of Islam claiming responsibility for violence, the Pope proposes a discourse about their validity in a forum where no one is threatened for suggesting that this question needs attention.

Basically, I think that the Pope did a great service, both to the free world and to Islam itself, to bring up this precise quandary about rationality. I have noticed over recent years that often, when this or the previous pope has received the credentials of a new ambassador from a Muslim state, he has delicately brought up the question of religious freedom with the implicit questioning of the status of non-Muslim believers in Muslim states. Why is it reasonable, after all, to allow new mosques to be built all over the world with Arab money but almost never allow Christian churches either to be built or to be guaranteed its freedom to worship in peace?

One can only say, furthermore, that the widespread hostile reaction to the Pope's university lecture seemed to most people to be precisely "irrational." Surely, this is not the impression Islam wishes to present before the world, even if it is explained in terms of obedience to Allah. It is an attempt to impose a rigid view of academic and intellectual investigation on everyone in the world so that no reasonable discussion about the truth of these tenets is allowed. No academic or intellectual space exists in which to examine the truth of a claim. We have only violence in enforcing its stated and unexamined position. The Pope's initiative made it clear, by the response to it, as nothing else does or can, that the political and ordinary culture of Islam has little place within it for a reasonable discussion of the truth of its own tenets. I suspect that the mere fact of the Pope's initiative in questioning the rationality of this religious system will have its eventual effect in Islam itself. The Pope, after all, does think this issue need not be solved violently. His inquiry about what Islam holds about itself is a genuine effort to find out how it understands its own claim to truth. It is an initiative that deserves something more than simple protest or threats.

An Islam that bases itself on a voluntarist proposition can only require obedience of its followers, not intellectual agreement nor rational obedience. What else can one conclude from reaction to a scholarly invitation to discuss the truth of its own clearly stated positions? If Islam is a true religion, as it claims to be, it cannot avoid the effort to explain why to the rest of the world. Or we might put the issue in a reverse fashion. Assuming that within Muslim life and philosophy, a significant number of its adherents do *not* agree that voluntarism in all its ramifications is the basis for the dignity and actions that many Muslim thinkers use to justify terrorists; why are these same Muslims not effective in pursuing the rationality issue against the terrorists? Why is there not more vigorous opposition to the terrorists among them? One reason, as is widely believed, may be simple fear of the ferocity of the terrorist wing especially against Muslim dissidents themselves. This is an issue that by itself brings up the question of the place of legitimate force in all of this discussion of the need of dialogue. Places of serious conversation need themselves to be protected with sufficient force to allow them to proceed.

II.

After the Pope had discussed voluntarist aspect of understanding this problem, he turned to the origins of the rational element. The Emperor had affirmed, from the Christian viewpoint, that "God is not pleased by blood" (#13). Indeed, he added that "not acting according to reason is contrary to God's nature." Where did a Byzantine Emperor get these ideas? The Pope then sketches the two sources of this understanding. One is Greek, the other is biblical. The two already in Mohammed's time, let alone in the Emperor's time, had a long interrelationship. There is a "harmony between what is Greek in the best sense of the word and the Biblical understanding of faith in God" (#17). The word "harmony" already indicates that things not the same somehow belong together in a higher whole.

The principal issue that concerns the Pope is the status of reason within Hebrew and Christian Scriptures, which are themselves admittedly not philosophical tractates. "What has Athens to do with Jerusalem?" (Tertullian) is a question going back to the beginnings of Christianity. The Pope, at this point, does a remarkable thing. He intimates that both in the Old and the New Testaments there are intimations of reason. Leo Strauss, Leon Kass, and Thomas Pangle have done important work to show how, even in spite of its concern with obedience to Yahweh, who Himself almost at times seems to be an Allah whose will is wholly arbitrary, the sacrifice of Isaac often being used as the classic case, there are definite intimations of reason throughout the history and texts of Israel. Much more is this reference to reason so in the New Testament. Clearly, Augustine, Aquinas, and the central line of Christian thinkers have accepted that there is an order in God, in the cosmos, and in man, an order that is, intrinsically, not arbitrarily but essentially related.

To establish the point of his reflections here, that *logos*, reason, is intrinsic to revelation itself as well as to philosophy, the Pope relates the first verse of Genesis to the Prologue of the Gospel of John (#17). Both passages are, at least in Christian theology, related to each other. Genesis tells us that "in the beginning" God created the "heavens and the earth." Heaven and earth, by themselves or together, are not God, not *all that is*. What were not God, the heavens and the earth, were, however, created to be "good." The good and the true are related, are signs of each other; they are not chaos. This passage is not unrelated to what the Pope will say later in the lecture about the goodness of science and its basis, its Platonic basis (#59).

The Gospel of John, however, takes this passage in Genesis to its roots. It intimates that the order found in creation does not originate with creation as some kind of self-designating intelligence. "In the beginning was *Logos*, the Word." This is the beginning before the beginning. This is to say that the order of cosmos presupposes the internal order within the Godhead. This is the doctrine of the Trinity not found in Islam. "*Logos* means both reason and word – a reason which is creative and capable of self-communication, precisely as reason" (#17). Whatever has *logos* can thus be receptive to word. Word depends on *what* is. Obedience to God cannot contradict the Word. Obedience is receptive to the "self-communication" of Reason to reason.

Greek philosophy at its best is necessary to and part of the faith. This does not mean that philosophy is "revealed" in Scripture. In that case, it would no longer be philosophy. Rather what is meant is that philosophy is needed to understand revelation. It gives us the tools by which we can accept its veracity, or at least see it is not contradictory. Nor did we give it to ourselves, but discovered it already intrinsic to our being. This view does not diminish but enhances the truth of God, Who is able to create beings that are themselves endowed with reason.

Augustine, Aquinas, and other philosophers used the very wording and understanding of Yahweh's definition of Himself in Exodus as "I Am." The Johannine gloss in the Prologue recalls that, in the beginning, God "created the heavens and the earth," as it says in Genesis. But, as it says in the Prologue, the world was not created before the Word, which was itself uncreated. The origin of world is, in fact, Word. This statement is not blasphemy but an affirmation of what God is.

This reflection brings us to the heart of the Regensburg Lecture. The expectation that God will not violate reason is based on the view that He will not contradict Himself. Some Muslim theologians do hold this view also, that if Allah is reasonable, he will not change his mind. The principle of non-contradiction is the essence of what it is to be reasonable. This emphasis on mind or intelligence does not mean that human minds are "equal" in power to the divine mind, or even to each other. It means, rather, that mind is found in all that God accomplishes outside of Himself. And this outside is reflective of His inner order. In this context, we cannot help but recall at this point the delight that Socrates, whom the Pope cites twice in this lecture, realized when he heard that "mind" was what was behind all things (Phaedo, 97c).

But this reliance on reason is an act of bravery on the part of the Pope. He understands the danger, even political danger, of any system that affirms that God can make evil good and good evil. In a sense, in this lecture at Regensburg, the Pope is absolutely unarmed. He postulates that Islam itself is challenged by its own claims, by the need to defend or deny in reason that God can command what is evil to be good. He does not want this issue to be decided in the streets, though its need of a decision on this score may be most manifest there. The truth of the issue must first be decided amidst the dons. He must find a place where what is held to be true can be accurately stated. We have seen that even when stated, it will not always or even often be responded to or accepted in reason or with reason. But the bravest act of our time is the act that insists, in a public university lecture, that what is unreasonable must defend itself in reason.

III.

At this point, the Pope brings up what is said in the Acts of the Apostles where Paul is called to go over into Macedonia instead of going farther into Asia (16, 6–10). Was pointing Paul in the direction of Greece rather than east, north, or south merely a question of chance? Was it somehow an "insult" to those living in these other directions? Must it be considered a sign of unconcern for other peoples or even prejudice against them? Or perhaps, in the long run, granted the missionary nature embedded in Christianity itself, the move to Greece was designed as the best way ultimately to reach other peoples. This purpose was not something that could become manifest in the short run.

At first sight, this reference to Macedonia might make us think that we are also at the first time that Greek and Christian thought meet. But, no, already in Jewish tradition perhaps the most important encounter with reason has already taken place. "The mysterious name of God, revealed from the burning bush, a name which separates this God from all other divinities with their many names and simply declares 'I am,' already presents a challenge to the notion of myth, to which Socrates' attempts to vanquish and transcend myth stands in close analogy" (#20). We do well to pay close attention to this important passage.

The first thing we notice is that gods that cannot be identified as "I am" are separated from this God *who is*. Secondly, the Socratic effort to vanquish "myth," must be in the name of a certain reality, in the name of "I am." The "myth," in its ultimate meaning, is a description of reality that does not literally conform to reality. The philosophic Averröists even held that the Koran itself was a "myth" designed to keep the people content and at bay. The philosophers, meantime, who could not accept its literal meaning, had access to a higher reality that was not subject to the Allah of the Koranic myth. The "truth" of the Koran and the "truth" of philosophy could contradict each other. But that contradiction was only known to the wise, who externally, at least, observed the Law. Yet they believed that only philosophy brought them to reality.

Socrates, for his part, saw myths as lies. He wanted to turn our souls to the good, to reality, to *what is*. This reality turn is why, in this context, the name given to Yahweh in Exodus, the "I am," is of such decisive importance. Being is not beyond being. The significance of the name of God as "I am" is that it precludes that the account of reality in revelation is mere myth. Rather, the name is a genuine address to philosophy, when philosophy is itself philosophy. And this understanding is where the Greeks come in.

The Pope observes that the God who identifies Himself as "I am" almost mocks the gods made of human hands (#21, Psalm 115). The great human question is not only "is God?" It is also, how are we properly to respond to Him because *He is*? It is the lesson of both philosophy and the Old Testament that this proper response to God is not something that is fabricated with our own hands or minds. Philosophy can, but should not, lead to idolatry. The desperate effort of the Hellenistic rulers to guarantee worship and to secure their rule by divinizing themselves is noted (#22). This divinization caused considerable persecution to the early Christians as well as in the Old Testament, as with the Maccabees.

Yet, the divinized emperors, in their attempt to stabilized political rule, were not the only story of this era. It was precisely during this latter period that Greek thought and the Old Testament revelation initially encountered each other through the Septuagint translation of the Old Testament (#23). This translation, Benedict says, "was decisive for the birth and spread of Christianity." How so? It was because the essence of Greek thought and the essence of revelation met each other here. Some moments in history are thus more significant than others, granted that divine providence is present in all time and place. This early encounter of Greece and Hebrew thought is why Manuel II "was able to say: Not to act 'with *logos* is contrary to God's nature'" (#24). The term *logos* was found in the Greek translation. It was understood after the manner of the "I am." Word and being were joined in the culture itself. What was new was not a contradiction of what was already present.

Thus, at least one understanding of God was not open to the idea that God could approve violence and still be God. But a second understanding of God, when spelled out, could present piety as obedience to and worship of a god that did approve violence. This view would take the form of never questioning whether what God was supposed to have commanded was, in fact, reasonable or not. In the voluntarist supposition of the essence of God as will, it was legitimate (one cannot say "rational," as that "category" cannot be applied to God in this understanding) to obey whatever is commanded or ordered to achieve the end. Indeed, in this obedience, one is said to show the highest reverence to the gods.

To recall an example of this mode of thought, though the Pope did not mention them by name, we might take the instance of the suicide bombers. The suicide bombers, in principle, are the most apt modern analogates to Manuel II's query about whether violence is permitted in the name of religion. The suicide bombers are living proof that the question of the religious legitimacy of violence is not simply a historical one. What is the "theology," the explanation, of their acts that motivate the suicide bombers? They are not precisely like Japanese Kamikaze pilots during World War II, seeking to destroy enemy warships by diving into them strapped to a bomb. Nor, though closer, are they like Buddhist monks who burn themselves to death in protest to some policy during the Vietnamese War. The Buddhist monk intends to kill no one but himself. He is pictured as a kind of flaming self-sacrifice or immolation.

From the "rational" point of view, the suicide bombers, at the same time, do two of the most terrible, that is, "irrational," acts in human civilization. First, they deliberately kill themselves. Evidently, there are "schools" throughout the Muslim world that teach young men and women both the morality and means to do this suicide killing in the most effective political manner. Mothers even kill their children along with themselves for this cause. Suicide bombing is a violation of the first principle that killing oneself is the most radical denial of the meaning of personal existence. But secondly, this self-murder, in its very purpose, also kills a certain number of others, however feasible at the moment. This, to the victims, unexpected and arbitrary killing is designed to create fear and chaos.

The suicide bombers are told and evidently believe that their act of killing themselves and others is an act of obedience to Allah. It thus subjectively is said to have a noble motive. As a result, their act, often erroneously, is called "martyrdom." The bombers themselves will, because of it, go to heaven and see Allah. Who do the bombers kill besides themselves? If accidentally they also kill other good Muslims, they too will go to heaven. Most people, however, call those killed by suicide bombers "innocent." However, like the Japanese pilot, the suicide bomber evidently thinks, or claims to think, that he is killing an enemy. Everyone not Muslim is, in such a view, an enemy.

Thus, elaborately drawn, centuries-old efforts to distinguish innocent and combatants in wartime are simply declared inoperative here. Once everyone is an enemy, there can remain no scruple about killing anyone if such violence is "reasonable" in fostering the religion. The suicide bomber, far from being considered an outcast, is a hero, deserving of honor. Those killed deserved to be killed. The precise point of the irrationality in this case is the claim that everyone not a Muslim is guilty and therefore an object of the ongoing war between Islam and its enemies.

But if it is not "reasonable" to kill the innocent, then

their arbitrary killing over recent decades by suicide bombers requires in the future judicial, police, and military forces to prevent these acts. If free society is to survive, these suicide bombers can neither be tolerated nor ignored. On the part of Islam itself, moreover, the suicide bombers demand an admission that such acts are in fact always and everywhere against reason. This must be the first request in reason to the question of redemption. The fate of the innocent cannot be that they deserve their fate because they are not Muslim. One might say, then, that the modern context of the suicide bomber killing innocent people in the name of religion is really not the praise of Allah but the question of redemption. This latter question seems implicit in the logic both of the question of who are killed by suicide bombers and of those who kill them. This issue seems to be intrinsic to and part of what Benedict is driving at in his initiative for a real dialogue about such fundamental issues.

This reasoning that justifies suicide bombers, its philosophical roots, is obviously contradictory to anything we know as a civilization of reason or love. We can, perhaps, admit that "subjectively" young suicide bombers, brought up in schools and within a culture that rewards and praises the act as noble, are, in Christian terms, "invincibly ignorant." But whether invincibly ignorant or fully believing that they are performing Allah's will, civil society must protect itself against these acts of violence. And the first step logically in this protection is to reject it as clearly "irrational," clearly against what God is. It is a dialogue about this position that the Regensburg Lecture is designed to initiate.

We can perhaps protect ourselves for a time from suicide bombers by jailing or eliminating those who seek to kill others. But the real problem is to change their minds. This is not unlike the old Donatist question that faced Augustine. The culture that fosters suicide bombing has to see and acknowledge the horror and irrationality of such terrible acts done in the name of religion. The issue that Manuel II talked about is, in principle, a pressing contemporary problem. The immediate pertinence of this question, I suspect, is why Benedict chose to use Manuel's reflection, relying on the intelligence of ordinary people to see the abidingness of principles over time.

IV.

At this point in his lecture, the Pope, evidently as an aside, but also as a forecast of the future not of Islamic civilization but of the West itself, drew a lesson from medieval philosophy and history. The understanding of Allah as pure will, as *voluntas ordinata*, was perfectly intelligible to those who had studied these ideas about God, reason, and will as they worked their way through the thought of the late Middle Ages. The primary author the Pope cites in this connection is Duns Scotus, though he might also have referred to William of Occam or Marsilius of Padua, even later Thomas Hobbes. Likewise, in addition to Ibn Hazm in the Muslim world, he could have cited al Ghazeli, al Ash'ari, or other more modern Muslim thinkers who explicitly or implicitly see the philosophic basis of the worldly mission of the Koran to be based on voluntarism.

This is not to say that there are no Muslim thinkers who followed Aristotle and strove to accept reason as the basis of action. But these latter do not finally seem prominent in Muslim religious circles that promote what we call terrorism. The Pope, like everyone else, might wish that they were. This is what his proposal for widespread discussion about the rationality of jihad, suicide bombing, and violence is about.

What concerns the Pope, however, is not merely the voluntarism in Islamic thought but the same system even in Christian thought. "In contrast with the so-called intellectualism of Augustine and Thomas, there arose with Duns Scotus a voluntarism which, in its later developments, led to the claim that we can only know God's *voluntas ordinata*. Beyond this is the realm of God's freedom, in virtue of which he could have done the opposite of everything he has actually done" (#25). The "opposite" of what God actually did does not mean that God might have created a different good world. That was in fact possible. Rather, it refers to the possibility of God's creating a world in which the principles of right and wrong were the exact opposite of what is the rule in this world, the rule of reason.

This view is near that of Ibn Hazm and, in its logic, could indicate a "capricious God" (#26). Such a God is one "not bound to truth and goodness." But we should appreciate the fact that this philosophical voluntarism is trying to protect God's transcendence and otherness. There is ample basis in the Old Testament itself, in its warnings about confusing God's ways with human ways, for appreciating the glimmer of truth in voluntarism. This is the basis of what is known as "negative theology." That is, to understand God and apply any concept to Him, we must first take all of our human notions and "purify" them. We must negate the human limitations found in them. Thus, our primary human understanding of God is not by directly knowing what He is in some sort of immediate vision. It consists in knowing what He is not.

This is how the Pope sees the danger of completely separating any common knowledge of God and reality: "God's transcendence and otherness are so exalted that our reason, our sense of the true and good, are no longer an authentic mirror of God, whose deepest possibilities remain eternally unattainable and hidden behind his actual decisions" (#26). In seeking to exalt God on the supposed basis of our own unknowing, we end up having no relation to Him at all.

What is to be done? At this point, Benedict cites authority, this time the authority of the Fourth Lateran Council, in 1215 (#27). Yet, he cited this authority for philosophic reasons, almost as if to say what Chesterton said, that oftentimes the purpose of authority in the Church is to save reason in the world. The transcendent nature of God is not to be conceived as resulting in a denial of any reason in ourselves. However more powerful and penetrating, reason in God does not deny reason in man, but implies it. Hence, it does not break the link between the highest power in God and man. "God does not become more divine when we push him away from us in a sheer, impenetrable voluntarism; rather, the truly divine God is the God who has revealed himself as *logos*, and as *logos* has acted and continues to act lovingly on our behalf" (#27).

Behind these remarks is a famous discussion about the relation of love and reason, something Benedict touched on in his *Deus Caritas Est*. There he was concerned to relate the Greek notion of *eros*, an outgoing, seeking love, with *agape*, a giving love. Aquinas has said that we possess the Beatific Vision finally through our reason, whereas the Scotists had stressed the primacy of love. Both are true in their own way. Indeed, Benedict, reconciling Augustine's restless heart as the basis of all of our longing for and seeking of beauty and good, finally maintained in his Encyclical that the power we have of *eros*, and we do have it, was first given to us. It was a gift designed itself to bring us to rest in an "I am" in which no more seeking is needed. Thus Benedict cites Paul in Ephesians (3:19) to the effect that love transcends knowledge, but he adds, "nonetheless, it continues to be love of the God who is *Logos*." What does this diversion on medieval voluntarism mean in terms of suicide bombers and modern thought? Nothing less than the fact that love and will cannot be totally separated from reason.

The Pope adds, following Paul's expression in Romans (12,1) concerning a "reasonable worship" that "Christian worship . . . is worship in harmony with the eternal Word and with our reason" (#28). In some small way, this short paragraph may be the most important one in the whole lecture. In the Roman canon, one of the adjectives used of Christ's sacrificial oblation in the Mass is *rationabilem*. If we read Catherine Pickstock's *After Writing*, Robert Sokolowski's *Eucharistic Presence*, or Joseph Ratzinger's *The Spirit of the Liturgy*, we will see precisely how the sacrifice of the New Law also relates to reason. The Mass is prohibited in various lands or neglected in others. Such deeds thus become not merely acts of force or simple negligences but a closing of the mind itself to *what is*. No single event in world history has stimulated more thought, more reason than the effort to understand the Mass, the memorial of Christ's death and resurrection. In this context, the effort to show as "unreasonable" not only the acts of terrorists and suicide bombers but also those that prevent the free saying and attending of Mass in the world become more central issues of reasoned discussion than we might at first anticipated.

The Pope, therefore, recognizes the world scope of that which he is about in this lecture. "The inner rapprochement between Biblical faith and Greek philosophical inquiry was an event of decisive importance not only from the standpoint of the history of religions, but also from that of world history" (#29). Christopher Dawson has often said that the single most important thing necessary to understand a culture is its religion. What Benedict is arguing in his Regensburg Lecture is that the culture that already contains within it the encounter of Greek philosophy and biblical faith has within itself a dynamic ferment that not only respects philosophy and reason, but fosters it.

But it can only do this if philosophy be philosophy, if its own theoretic principles are sufficient to understand what it is. The efforts to praise God by exalting Him beyond reason end up, if not careful, eliminating reason. This elimination is what we are seeing before our eyes. No one but the Pope seems to be telling us to think about what we are doing, and not doing.

Chapter III.

WHAT IS EUROPE?

"The encounter between the Biblical message and Greek thought did not happen by chance. The vision of St. Paul, who saw the roads to Asia barred and in a dream saw a Macedonian man plead with him: 'Come over to Macedonia and help us!' (Acts, 16, 6–10) – this vision can be interpreted as a 'distillation' of the intrinsic necessity of a rapprochement between Biblical faith and Greek inquiry" (#19).

"This inner rapprochement between Biblical faith and Greek philosophical inquiry was an event of decisive importance not only from the standpoint of the history of religions, but also from that of world history – it is an event which concerns us even today. Given this convergence, it is not surprising that Christianity, despite its origins and some significant developments in the East, finally took on its historically decisive character in Europe" (#29).

I.

In a striking affirmation, Benedict XVI, in his Regensburg

Lecture, brings up the whole Augustinian question of the theology of history. A theology of history would mean a description of the meaning of historical events as they are found in the books of revelation. What is this meaning? What are the events that accomplish it? Why is the Incarnation at a given place and at a given time significant? Certainly, Scripture in various ways does indicate that there is a beginning, middle, and end to the existence of man in the world and of the world itself. While there are cyclic elements in it, the course of world history in Scripture is linear in this sense. What seems most to confound us about it is its scope both in time and space as concentrated in events on this planet.

In one sense, Scripture teaches us that God knew us, both individually and collectively, before we were, and He will be with us beyond this world. Here the word "end" can have two meanings. One meaning indicates purpose; the other meaning designates the termination of a temporal sequence. This "termination," moreover, can be conceived as a disaster or as the final blossoming out into what was intended to be permanent, the peaceful City of God. Probably no one has thought more about time and man's place within it than Augustine. Augustine himself was studied by Joseph Ratzinger, whose doctoral dissertation was on the very idea of the City of God in Augustine. Few passages are more interesting in the Regensburg Lecture than this one about the meaning of our temporal existence in this world.

Augustine tells us that he wrote the longest (1200

pages) of his many works, *The City of God*, because he was asked by a certain Marcellus to defend Christians against the contemporary Roman accusation that the conversion of Rome to Christianity was the cause of its political downfall. When the Romans ceased worshipping their founding gods, these gods abandoned them. This cultic abandonment was the "cause" of their political problems. The pagan Romans evidently thought that the gods were behind their astonishing record of conquest and rule in the ancient world. Augustine did not think these gods were gods.

Augustine would have none of this thesis, of course. He pointed out that most of Rome's moral problems already existed before Christianity ever came on the scene. If Rome was in trouble, it was caused by its own failure to observe the decencies already depicted and defined by the pagan philosophers. Many Christian writers previous to Augustine, like Eusebius and Orosius, had in fact claimed to see some providential purpose could be found in the events surrounding the birth and death of Christ. A kingdom of God was somehow being established on this earth. What happened was merely a substitution of the Roman gods by the Christian God.

Augustine, however, did not think this change of belief would ever result in a perfect kingdom in this world. The world, for as long as it lasted, would be hard pressed to be anything but a vale of tears. While he thought that by living rightly and quietly, some improvement in this world might be made, Augustine ever stands on that side of the political insight that affirms, because of its deep insight into sin and fallen human nature, that we should always be also prepared for the worst. Augustine does not locate finally our ultimate happiness in some earthly political kingdom, nor does he think this worldly kingdom is what our life on earth is about, even if it is the context of the central drama of how we relate ourselves to God though our understandings and choices.

The true destiny of Christ's followers was beyond this life. Still their status in this transcendent life has much to do with how we lived in this world. Politics, economics, and the affairs of state were, at first sight, merely ways of passing the time until the real world of our end was given to us in the final Judgment. Augustine, however, was not a pessimist. Quite the contrary, he wrote the *City of God* primarily to locate the real "city in speech," about which Socrates had spoken in the *Republic*. He concludes that it was "real." It was neither a final kingdom in this world nor was it merely a philosophic idea. Any attempt to claim that men by their own powers could create in this world what men really looked for with the aid of grace was not only folly, but dangerous. Augustine's political realism was an anti-utopian tract. It warned us about looking for our final meaning in the wrong way or in the wrong place.

Yet, paradoxically, no one was more influential than Augustine and his great book in implanting in our souls, in the soul of Western culture itself, the idea that we could in this world, by living a worthy life, make things better than they were. And this "improvement," even by worldly standards, would be a direct result, even in reason, of the initiatives put into the world through the impetus of revelation, particularly the notion of sacrifice, charity, innocent suffering, and careful reasoning. Indeed, up until relatively modern times, the civilization that resulted from the confluence of Jerusalem, Athens, and Rome was simply called "Christendom." It was a civilization in which its ideas and institutions were worked out not so much when reason and revelation were seen to be disharmonious to each other, but when they were seen as a coherent whole that itself distinguished what belonged to reason, what to politics, what to grace.

This "Western" civilization, no doubt, found its beginning in the famous defeat of the Persians at Marathon and Salamis by the Greeks from Sparta and Athens, as Herodotus tells us. Moreover, from its inception, Christendom always had, and still retains, an old East and, after the conversion of Russia, a new East. But it also had a South in the north of Africa from whence Augustine himself came. Christendom was largely the world around the Mediterranean, a Latin speaking and a Greek speaking division. The waves of invasion from the Eurasian plain, from the Huns, the Lombards, the Vikings, the Vandals, Magyars, and the rest, with their own customs, yet with their desire to become civilized, that is, to become Roman, provided the configuration that we came to know as Europe. Nothing was more important in establishing this European identity than the appearance in the seventh and eighth centuries of Muslim armies in the south. These armies quickly succeeded in overrunning a good part of the south, east, and even the west of Europe, in Spain and the Islands of the Mediterranean.

All through the Middle Ages, the Muslim culture was said to be superior in grandeur and sophistication to that of the more "barbarian" Europe. Muslim armies seemed almost invincible and, but for two fortunate battles, one at Tours in the eighth century and one at Vienna in the seventeenth, they almost succeeded in conquering the north of Europe itself. The Crusades were not, as is often claimed, a sign of innate aggressiveness on the part of Christianity. Rather, they were a belated, almost desperate endeavor to prevent the Europeans themselves from being conquered by the ever-aggressive Islam. The strange decline in early modern times of Muslim power, though not its culture, within its domain, has long been a topic of speculation, particularly its record in the advances in modern science and economy. In 1938, Belloc predicted at the end of his book on the Crusades that should Islam ever again acquire the power, it would continue on its earlier conquests. In retrospect, these words seem rather prophetic.

II.

What we now think of as Europe is the continent that is currently organizing itself, unifying itself from Spain to Greece and Turkey, to the very frontiers of Russia. It is now officially conceived to be a wholly secular culture to the seemingly deliberate exclusion of its Christian origins, that began in its present form in the Middle Ages. It was in that period that began the civilization that we now describe as "modern." It is a world of technology, science, freedom, leisure. Many even want to replace the term, "modern," with "post-modern" because of the radical differences in conception of human purpose and human person that now seem to motivate the people in Europe. The spiritual remains of Christian culture that went along with the aftermath of the two great wars of the twentieth century are largely gone. Already after World War I, we heard themes of "the decline of the West." Many books in the 1940s, however, thought the time was ripe for a reaffirmation of Christian and rational culture, as was the case after the fall of Communism in 1989.

Yet, today Europe seems in many ways to be dying. Even without war, one might almost say especially without war, its citizens are being replaced often, ironically, by more birth-inclined Muslim peoples. These people are more and more needed for labor and services to a rapidly aging population. European military impotence, as well as the impotence of its political will, seems also related to its demography. All through recent decades, ironically, it was the papacy, much to the consternation of almost everybody, including Catholics, that took the lead in warning of the disastrous results of this anti-natal mentality, something everywhere visible today, though few want to examine its spiritual causes.

The present pope is himself a German. He is someone from the heart of the troubled Europe of the twentieth century. His elevation to the papacy calls our attention, in a graphic way, to the question of what is Europe. Likewise, it emphasizes the weak condition of Christianity within this Europe. But the German Pope also takes us back to the earlier question of Paul's call to come over into Macedonia to help the people there. Within this Europe, of course, even from its philosophic roots in the Greeks and its political roots in the Romans, the people who identified their city with the world, the question of whether it will manage to survive remains an open question. It is surprising the number of writers who think it is already too late, spiritually too late, demographically too late.

The Holy Father suggests in his lecture that the confrontation between Christian revelation and Greek philosophy was no mere "accident," but a step in providence itself. What can we make of this observation? For some centuries, now, we have followed many studies about the "de-christianization" or secularization of Europe and the West. Spengler's post-World War I book, *The Decline of the West*, still haunts. Writers like Christopher Dawson (*The Making of Europe*), Harold Berman (*Law and Revolution: The Formation of the Western Legal Tradition*), and Josef Pieper (*Scholasticism*), among others, however, had shown how Europe is the product of a coherent fusion of Hebrew, Greek, Roman, and Christian thought together with the lived experiences of its ancient and medieval heritage. Most argue also that it was precisely the success of the Muslim armies in former Roman Empire territories that finally turned Europe in on itself to develop its own separate culture.

What the Pope sees as making this separate culture most what it is comes from what he calls "a profound harmony." Europe, the home later on of the classical symphony, has its origin in the harmonious relationship to two things that at first sight seem incompatible. This same harmony was also, in the Pope's earlier comment, what was at the heart of the idea of a university (#5). "I believe that here we can see the profound harmony between what is Greek in the best sense of the word and the Biblical understanding of faith in God" (#17). Obviously, the Pope, who has studied its history, knows that certain things also appear in Greek philosophy "in the worst sense of the word." This comparison harkens back to a further question of whether in its relation to Greek thought itself, Christian thinkers, notably Augustine and Aquinas, were themselves genuinely philosophical. This philosophy, it turns out, was itself more philosophical precisely because of its need to consider the content and implications of revelation. The deepest roots of the university and even the Regensburg Lecture lie here. The fact is that Plato and Aristotle were not used simply as "authorities" on philosophy but as themselves philosophers. And they were understood and used because of philosophy itself, not because they were exemplars of Platonic or Aristotelian philosophy. Philosophy was the search for truth, not for who said it.

The Pope again, in relation to Scripture, refers to "the best of Greek thought" (#22). This encounter occurs at a "deep level." This encounter is seen in the "wisdom literature" of the Old Testament. Its result, he tells us, is "mutual enrichment of both." One of the constant themes in Christian thought on philosophy, science, and revelation is that the excellence of every legitimate inquiry is improved when both reason and revelation are included. Benedict's abiding theme is that reason is not something totally separate from, hostile to, or contradictory of faith. Perhaps what is most striking about these remarks is that Christianity seems to have a vested interest not only that revelation be revelation, but that philosophy be philosophy. In Christianity, any thought of a "two truth" theory, that is, a truth of reason can contradict a truth of revelation, is excluded as inherently heterodox. Why? Because Christian revelation does not allow it to imagine that Christ did not actually exist, nor does it, subsequently, allow the mind, that is, philosophy, the possibility of denying the existence of what does in fact exist or our ability to know reality through the powers inherent in us.

In speaking of Manuel II's own implicit assimilation both of Greek reason and biblical faith, joined together in one coherent whole, the Pope even uses the expression "from the heart of Christian faith" to the "heart of Greek thought" (#25). These two elements now manifest a "distinct step in the history of revelation." Something comes to be in time that was not there before. The dynamic movement of history does happen because of events that happen within it that we are constrained to recognize precisely as having really happened even if they have to do with revelation. Our philosophy is thus filled with *what is*.

It should be noted, in this connection, that John Paul II's instruction on Catholic universities was called precisely *"Ex Corde Ecclesiae."* That is, the university itself as we know it in this culture was called forth not by itself nor from the state, but from the heart of the Church. Do universities which do not understand themselves as so conceived see themselves open to the whole truth? Do they become merely what are now called "politically correct" institutions? In this sense, the Regensburg Lecture is not only given at a university, but it is addressed *to* the university, to its heart, to what it is intended to be. It is not so clear that such a question about the whole can be posed in universities found under Islamic or Western sponsorship – some, alas, would even worry about those claiming "Catholic" sponsorship.

As we have mentioned, the Pope actually maintains that this "event" of the mind, this inner seeing of the relationship of the strand of faith and that of reason was and still is a factor in "world history" (#29). The "event," once put into existence, is still going on. What can this mean? First of all, the subject matter of this "event" is the "inner rapprochement," the putting together and the keeping together of both reason and revelation. This ongoing historical presence must mean that precisely this "inner rapprochement" is designed for more than Europe, however much it informed what it is to be Europe. In our era, we hear it argued that the world is filled with a number of separate "cultures," more or less closed off from one another, in spite of the famous "globalization." The adequacy and limits of this multi-cultural concept will be what the Pope will talk about when he comes to his third mode of dehellenization.

But Christianity cannot conceive itself to be a one-culture religion, even if it also represents the universal culture, both in philosophy and in revelation. What the Pope is concerned about here, then, in his "event" emphasis within the actual "history" of mankind is that this "inner rapprochement" be allowed and encouraged to enter freely into all places where the dignity and intelligence of our kind are to be found. Ultimately, this is what the Church's modern emphasis on human dignity and religious freedom in all polities and cultures has been about.

Benedict recognizes that, in fact, this cultural openness is not the case often in theory, more often in practice. One of the reasons why he, at this point, is so much concerned with "reason" is because that is the one agreed-upon basis on which, in logic, all must discourse. Even when "reason" is not recognized as a criterion, as is sometimes the case in Islam with its voluntarism and in the West with its unlimited "rights-talk," both dialectically and logically all such difference must try to give an account of the legitimacy of their stand. This is appealing to reason, whatever it be called. This reason classically deals at a fundamental level with what cannot be otherwise. It is at this level that the notion of the reasonableness of "violence" must be confronted.

How are we to read the Pope's remark about Europe as the locus of this mutual acceptance of faith and reason? The Old Testament notion of a "chosen people" is sometimes interpreted as a kind of prejudice of Yahweh against other peoples. To be sure, almost every people, beginning with the ancient Chinese, have exclusive conceptions of themselves. One's own uniqueness is itself part of the meaning of universal humanity. But this historical attention to what happened in Europe indicates that within Europe already an openness was found that did not yet exist elsewhere. Literally, because of Greek philosophy "at its best," it was possible actually to see and understand in a manner that was not in fact possible with other philosophic presuppositions. Ultimately, this relationship implies a reasonable approach to other cultures when the political occasion is such that the issue of what is true and what is not true in other cultures can be safely asked.

III.

Is this turn to Europe, then, an "exclusiveness" that denigrates the genius of myriads of other peoples, historical and present? Here is what Benedict says: "given this convergence, it is not surprising that Christianity, despite its origins and some significant development in the East, finally took on its historically decisive character in Europe" (#29). One could read this passage two ways. There is first an "inner warning" that Europe's own spiritual condition is so precarious that the basis of this rapprochement of reason and faith is disappearing. As a result, the rest of the world is in danger of losing the prime image of what it means for reason and revelation to belong to the same discourse. A second way to read it would be to suggest that something obviously distinct happened in Europe precisely because of the "inner rapprochement" that the Pope is describing.

In divine providence, the choice of Europe first was

not arbitrary but in fact the easiest and most gentle way, should Europe be loyal to its founding, to insert this truth of the inner coherence in all cultures. Fundamentally, there can be nothing wrong with implying that all cultures, no matter how diverse, have or ought to have some fundamental things in common. A part of what happened when this synthesis was intact is shown by results in the success of science and technology. Everyone in all the cultures seeks to imitate this side of Europe, even though once such science and method are discovered and known, no science or method as such is national or cultural.

One of the things to note about particularly Christian revelation is that it does not itself have a political philosophy other than the notion of things of God and things of Caesar. Both the Old Testament and Islam are law states when perfected and put into effect. Christianity, by not having a political program, implicitly acknowledged that the proper knowledge of political things, as derived from living experience by the philosophers and politicians, was itself legitimate. In this sense, discussion of the proper organization of political things is a work of reason, practical reason. A religion or ideology that finds the proper political forms outside of reason will, generally speaking, not allow the institutions of reason or of the economy to exist in their most open and free condition. This lack of an independent political philosophy is in part why it is so difficult not only to dialogue but to live freely in many cultures. Even the most basic freedoms and dignities are controverted, such as even having a Bible.

The fact is that it was in Greece where the notions of what it is to be political were most coherently worked out. Aristotle already has a distinction between the theoretical and practical orders. What was to be done in this world by the mortal being as mortal was basically understood by the Greeks. They understood the different kinds of souls likely to be formed by differing choices of ends or definitions of happiness.

What they did not know, as both Augustine and Samuel Johnson later pointed out, was how actually to be virtuous. But what the various natural virtues were, this was already known to the philosophic Greeks and recalled by Cicero. Revelation does not really improve on Greece's basic understanding of the virtues. This fact indicates that revelation begins with the fact that the human being as such is good. The point that needs to be made here is that, for all its defects, particularly the problems that arise when both Greece after Alexander and Rome after Caesar divinized their rulers, the turn to Europe made sense from the point of view of the inner coherence of the Greek mind and revelation. It was not necessarily a turn "against" Asia or Africa or anyone else. It was a historical turn to reason that was part of an announced mission "to go forth and teach all nations."

That goal was the teaching all nations by another means, perhaps a less direct, but more effective, route. Indeed, to extend this teaching to all nations, to instruct them in what it was they yet needed to know to understand themselves, their final destiny, included activities that they themselves, in their human qualities, participated in. In this sense, the later development of what we know as science and technology may well be related to this same turn. This story of course is not yet complete. But this possibility is no doubt why the Pope saw it proper to spend considerable time in putting our understanding of science in its proper place. Belloc in fact thought that much of the dynamism of Islam to conquer the world came from this same inspiration found first among the Christians. It is in this context of interest that the question of why science died in the Islamic world in modernity relates to the question of whether science needs certain anterior theological propositions among which is the permanency of secondary causes and the usefulness of investigating a nature that will not be otherwise. The extensive inclusion of the basis of science in this lecture, thus, is not accidental.

In other writings, Benedict has shown considerable interest in the question of what Europe is. What he seeks to accomplish in this lecture is to "understand" Europe in such a way that its self-rejection of the basic principle that actually formed it is a species of cultural suicide. Near the end of the lecture, Benedict states: "the West has long been endangered by this aversion to the question which underlies its rationality, and can only suffer great harm thereby" (#62). But has Europe and the civilization it spawned given up rationality? The suspicion, indeed the certainty, that, in large part, it has, at its deepest core, explains both Benedict's initial "turn" to consider Islam, then his second turn back to Europe.

Just what does Benedict mean when he says that the West is "endangered" by its own philosophic understanding of what it means by rationality? The Pope goes into this question in tracing what is generally called the history of modernity. This is the human project that affirms that man is understood only by pursuing what are called "scientific" means. The question is, are there relevant and real things in existence that we do not see because we do not want to see them? Is our problem with the "rationality" or lack of it? Is Islam itself a product of a form of reasoning that prevents us from seeing the whole of *what is*, of what happens to our kind?

One of the most memorable passages in my reading of Alexander Solzhenitsyn during the worst of the Communist era was his description of what was printed in mimeographed *samizdat* papers. These papers were hastily written, dangerously distributed accounts of a myriad of individual incidents that actually happened every day in the police state that was the Soviet Union. Hannah Arendt later, in her *Human Condition*, and Yves Simon in his *A General Theory of Authority*, reduced this experience to the dimensions of essentially Aristotelian thought, that is, to the Greek mind. Things that happen every day in the world's streets cannot be deduced from some *a priori* principles. Speaking of what he called "witnesses," Simon said that the witness may be obliged simply to tell the truth of what he saw. He was the only one present on that corner of a particular day when some terrible event happened. If we are to know such a truth, it is only by testimony of an honest witness.

Solzhenitsyn recognized that torture and police tactics could terrify people into "forgetting" or lying about what they saw. So if a certain family or individual was rounded up and taken to prison, there would be no record of this event unless someone carefully, with attention to time, place, and circumstances, recorded exactly what happened. The witness became the only person who could state what really happened. It might be dangerous to tell this truth. But our knowledge of what happened depended upon this testimony.

In the case of contemporary Islamic terrorist violence, we are, in the service of reason, likewise in dire need of a similar service. Each suicide bombing, each beheading, each torture must be carefully and exactly documented – where, to whom, by whom? Such events, of course, can terrify us. They are intended to terrify us into silence. But the point I am making here is that of the record of reason. What the Pope was after was this very service of reason in a time when irrationality and terror are looked upon as tools of religion or as methods of silencing opposition.

No doubt the same point can be made of the abortion killings and for the same reason. These killed human beings are demographically needed today. But they are not even acknowledged to have existed to be needed. The Pope does not deny that some force, both military and police, will also be needed. He knows that political realism also teaches that reason and its institutions have at times to be courageously defended. But his main thrust is to recall the real scope of reason in the culture. The scientific mind cannot justify itself in not facing such challenges to reason on the grounds of reason itself. The defense of Europe is likewise the defense of reason. But what seems to be even further implied by the "turn to Europe" is the historical mission initiated by Paul coming over to Macedonia. Europe's own intellectual crisis is a spiritual crisis for the rest of the world. For the other cultures to flourish properly, they too need to be what they potentially are – an infusion of this inner rapprochement that, like revelation and reason, is, in principle, universal and not simply European.

The German theologian Karl Adam once remarked that present within European reason is something also more than just human reason. Reason and revelation have here already encountered each other. But it is often a difficult thing, especially for what, as we will see, came to be called "modern man," to define himself in any terms other than those of his own self-creation. "Since the guilt of humanity culminates in the fact that man wishes to be nothing other than himself, nothing but what is purely human and natural, the Redeemer, since he will surrender himself as a redemption for mankind, now faces the whole, unrestrained power of the merely human."[1] The notion of the "merely human" is, of course, from Nietzsche, from his attack on Christianity as the ultimate weakness. Notice that it is precisely what Karl Adam called "the guilt of humanity" that causes man to wish for nothing other than himself.

1   Karl Adam, *The Son of Man* (Garden City, N.Y.: Doubleday Image, [1934], 1960), 225–26

The argument of Benedict, I think, is rather that there is nothing "guilty" at all in realizing that revelation addresses itself in our culture to reason, that to be given more than is due is neither a defect nor a fault. The mutual compatibility between the two, reason and revelation, granting their proper distinction, is the cause of the vitality of Europe. Paul turned to Greece because the Greek mind, "at its best," was there. That philosophy, even "at its best," still had much to learn, even about reason. This is the lesson that, as Aquinas recalled (I-II, 91, 4) in asking about the need of a divine law in addition to a natural and human law, needed to be understood. But the initial challenge of the turn to Europe was not merely to understand what man "naturally" was, but what he was intended to be in his actual creation, something more and higher than he might have expected by his own powers. Thus, Christendom, Europe, stood, not merely for philosophy but for both philosophy and revelation. And it pointed not merely to itself, but to any one, who like Paul, could plead for them to come over to help them. The ability to help was not spoken against philosophy, but with philosophy. The call of other Macedonias is itself part of the expectant element still vibrant in history, actual history.

At the intellectual origin of Europe we find two political trials, that of Socrates before the Assembly in Athens, and that of Christ before the Roman governor in Jerusalem. John Paul II had noted in *Crossing the Threshold of Hope* that these two trials seem to be related. Indeed, they both go to the heart of the basic question of all political philosophy and human living. Why do even the best cities kill the best men? Here we already have Athens, Jerusalem, and Rome bound together in the same ponderings. While Benedict twice refers to Socrates in the Regensburg Lecture, he does not specifically refer to these trials as themselves formative of the mind of Europe. Yet, it seems that it is precisely these trials that most set the agenda for the query Benedict did state to be the heart of his concern, namely, does violence promote religion. Both Socrates and Christ suffered violence. Contrary to Machiavelli, they were not unsuccessful prophets. They taught us that violence does not have the last word, even when it, by all earthly standards, appears to conquer.

Christ and Socrates were the unarmed prophets whose lesson Machiavelli was most concerned to eliminate from our souls, especially the souls of the potential philosophers. For he understood, as did Nietzsche later on, that it is above all their teaching that prevents religion or philosophy from being so used to promote violence. The paradox, of course, is that Socrates' "it is never right to do wrong" and Christ's innocent suffering and the forgiveness of enemies result in their deaths at the hands of the state. It is the lesson of these two trials that is embedded in the soul of Europe. It is this fact that Europe ever presents both to itself and to other cultures not as something peculiar to Europe but as something all must learn.

Chapter IV.

MODERNITY AND THE THREE WAVES OF DEHELLENIZATION

"The thesis that the critically purified Greek heritage that forms an integral part of Christian faith
has been countered by the call for a dehellenization
of Christianity – a call which has more and more
dominated theological discussions since the beginning of the modern age" (#31).

I.

The Pope's three steps in "dehellenization," the subject that
constitutes the latter part of the Regensburg Lecture,
sound like Leo Strauss's three "waves" of modernity. These
latter three waves, of course, themselves recall the three
"waves" in the fifth book of the *Republic*. A debate between
Joseph Ratzinger and Járgen Habermas was reported in *Le
Monde* (April 27, 2005). In it, Cardinal Ratzinger cited the
witticism of Strauss about the logical consequences of relativism as a philosophical position, that "if all positions are
of equal intellectual merit, then cannibalism is only a matter of taste." I suppose one could even wonder just what

cannibals taste when they taste something in their view edible. But the point about relativism is the same as the problem involved in the primacy of will, namely, that nothing objective exists to distinguish one view from another except power or choice or, yes, taste.

Strauss was famous for having succinctly formulated what most contemporary thinkers understand "modernity" or the "modern project" to be. Basically, its intelligibility goes back to the idea that reads, in Aquinas's formulation, *homo non proprie humanus sed superhumanus est* (man is not properly human but superhuman). In this understanding, natural man was never in fact created. What exists from the actual beginning was God's intention and carrying out of a plan in which man, whatever his own self-definition, was elevated to an end, the Beatific Vision of God, to which he could not aspire by the natural powers or end of what it is to be a human being. Yet, he could be so elevated to this purpose if God granted him the capacity. Aquinas' phrase means that this capacity was granted. Man as we know him is intended to a supernatural end. All his heart and desires tend in this direction. This tendency does not mean that he has no natural desires, nor does it mean that they are, as such, bad. Rather it means that through and beyond all that is good that he tends to, he nonetheless seeks what is properly the inner life of the Godhead as his final good.

The German theologian, Karl Adam, had written in 1934 of an adamant refusal on the part of man in his present status to acknowledge anything that was not exclusively human. God was felt to be alien, not the purpose of man's being. Indeed, the word "humanism" in some conceptions came to imply this same notion that only man knows what man is. In all relevant aspects in this understanding of modernity, man is created to be what he is by man, not God. Not only is "nothing human alien," but nothing higher than human has anything to teach us. Put in another fashion, it means that all causes are human causes. The practical intellect, contrary to the Greek priority, is superior to the theoretical intellect which, in this understanding, has no claim to our normative attention, especially in things that pertain to how we live, to what we are, to our ultimate destiny.

These latter ideas about the superiority of the practical intellect were rooted in Roman and modern Stoicism, in Marsilius of Padua, in Francis Bacon, in Rousseau. Such merely practical definitions of what we are, presupposed to nothing but ourselves, of course, deftly remove both revelation and natural law or reason from contention in considering what man is in reality. There is at work, in other words, a certain "reduction" or lowering of our sights. We no longer look to those divine and immortal things that Aristotle told us in book ten of the *Ethics* are our main delight, the things that could not be otherwise. Rather, as Benedict put it, we voluntarily refuse to admit anything but our own definitions and understandings of what it is to know the human (#40). Contrary to Aristotle, man *does* make man to be man. Humanism is defined against theism.

The Pope himself affirms, lest there be any doubt, that

there are in fact "positive aspects of modernity" that are to be "accepted unreservedly" (#54). This reaffirmation can only mean, of course, that what is in fact reasonable is perfectly acceptable when its truth is reasonably discovered or arrived at. Modernity is a problem not when it is reasonable in the broadest sense but when it narrows itself, in the very name of truth, so that it can see only a part of reality. It is the breaking of this inner coherence in the history of later Western thought, even beginning in the later Middle Ages, that is the origin of modernity as a problem and that defines its nature. The Regensburg Lecture is itself an examination of modernity in both the acceptable and dubious senses of the term. It is of particular interest to see just what in modernity that Benedict saves and why.

The Pope indicated that the first stage of modernity, in its inner intelligibility, concerns the Reformation. Again, as in the case of Islam, in delineating what he considers to be a crucial problem in modernity beginning in the Reformation, the Pope is not rejecting "ecumenism." Nor is he saying that the Reformation was terrible on every score. In an academic lecture, he takes the intellectual understanding of the Reformation seriously. He states how he understands the problem it posed. He is not reopening the religious wars of the sixteenth and seventeenth centuries. Nor is he claiming that Catholic theologians had no faults. He is trying to understand and articulate in intellectual terms what happened. He is aware that the philosophy and theology that buttressed the Reformation went back a long way. The Reformers themselves affirmed this antiquity.

Indeed, they claimed to return to Christian beginnings before philosophy was said to have come into Christian usage. Benedict has read his Luther, Calvin, and other reformers, as well as Occam and Duns Scotus, Aquinas and Augustine, indeed Plato and Aristotle along with the modern historians and critics.

Luther is famous for his generally negative attitude to both Aquinas and Aristotle. He had a reason for this opposition. He thought scholastic philosophy was so overloaded with philosophic explications that it obscured Scripture's original formulations. The Reformers thought that "they were confronted with a faith system totally conditioned by philosophy" (#31). This philosophy, being Greek and pagan, was "alien." The Pope explained that, to the Reformers, faith no longer "appeared as a living historical Word but as one element of an overarching philosophical system" (#33). In the Averröist system, of which this approach is uncomfortably mindful, the philosopher explained where faith fit into the system. Philosophy decided the place and validity of faith as such. In this system, the philosopher did not, as in, say, Aquinas, respond to what was found in revelation from its own living source. Understood this way, that philosophy absorbed faith, the Reformers were right. Philosophy had subsumed faith. But this was not what the central tradition held about the relation of faith and reason.

The famous phrase, *sola scriptura*, furthermore, sought a "pure" faith, one not encumbered by philosophy as if that were an abiding impediment, not an intrinsic necessity and freedom needed more fully to understand faith itself, as well as reason. But the "philosophy of Jesus," as Peter Kreeft has shown, is precisely one that requires the mind to acknowledge real things both as a starting point and as the source of new knowledge. If it cannot do this, not even Scripture's pure words are credible. "Seeing the lilies of the field, how they grow," is not after all an impediment to knowing what revelation is. For the Reformers, however, "metaphysics appeared as a premise derived from another source, from which faith had to be liberated in order to become fully itself" (#34). Metaphysics thus could not be a help to understanding what faith maintained about reality, including the reality of God. This separation left faith standing alone out there, itself indifferent to the presuppositions that were contained in the minds of those who heard it. Again this need of a realist philosophy may be one reason for the turn from Asia to Greece (#19). It is not an indifferent matter even for the faith what metaphysical understanding underlay what is heard as faith.

The Pope is quite aware of what is at stake here. He is not wrong to bring in at this point the figure of the great German philosopher Emmanuel Kant. It is important to point out to the tradition of the Reformers about *sola scriptura* that there is a problem with it. Gilson said somewhere that we are free to set down our own first principles, but once we set them down, we no longer think as we will but only as we can within the confines of our selected premises. Sooner or later, someone will draw the logical conclusions from our chosen first principles. Kant, some three hundred years after the Reformers, drew the conclusion. Kant, the Pope remarks, held that to protect the faith, not only must we set aside metaphysics, but we "needed to set thinking aside in order to make room for faith" (#35). This is a remarkable statement. Not "*credo ut intelligam*," but "*credo quia non cogito*" becomes the norm. Thinking and faith are precisely unrelated.

This eighteenth-century "radicalism," as the Pope called it, was perhaps something that the "Reformers could never have foreseen." But this unexpected conclusion does not mean that it was not in the logic of their initial desire to remove philosophy from its inner connection with our understanding of what faith might imply. The conclusion of Kant, separating them entirely, rather indicated the "profound harmony" that existed between faith and reason to which the Pope had already averred (#17). In the Catholic tradition, faith was not a rival to or alternative to reason. It was addressed to it as already an active power consciously and self-reflectively understanding as much as it could by its own powers. Reason had to be reason if revelation is to be revelation. Revelation is not an escape from reason nor a denial of it. It is a stimulus to it in its own depths.

What is the final result of the first "wave" of dehellenization in its "inner coherence?" The result is actually surprising. It follows the Stoics, Bacon, and the positivists, but it is phrased in Aristotelian language. Faith is now "anchored" in "practical reason," a most perceptive conclusion. What does this emphasis on practical reason mean? What follows? That faith, as such, has "no access to the whole." The faith only contacts what we make, whereas classical practical intellect understood that it presupposed something that it did not itself make in order for it to be what it is.

Of course, one good definition of philosophy itself might be "access to the whole." If faith deals only with what we do, with practical intellect, it can have nothing to do with what we are or what reality is, something about which we certainly would like to know. Kant's moral principles are postulates, not principles grounded in a nature that is itself the result of eternal law. Kant will ask us to be "moral" without our having any assurance in reality that being moral is true or not. It depends solely on the logic of the postulates or imperatives.[1]

Aristotle is quite clear that practical science is a good thing. But it is not the highest science, only a high science in its own practical order. Practical sciences need theoretical rectitude even to be themselves. Practical science, by being what it is, itself points beyond itself. We not only want to make well and to do well. We want to know that what we make and do is well, is good in itself, outside our own making. That latter assurance is the only reasonable motivation to do something in the first place, namely, because it is good. At the end of the first dehellenization, we are left with Scripture but no reason except as a postulate.

---

1 The best book that relates what is valid in Kant's practical intellect to Aristotle is Hadley Arkes, *First Things: An Inquiry into the First Principles of Morals and Justice* (Princeton N.J.: Princeton University Press, 1986).

This result cannot be the real way to foster and protect the faith, or even to act well on the pure inspiration of Scripture. Scripture itself presents us with problems that have to be authoritatively resolved, something scholastic philosophy understood and on which the authority of the Church was built.

Scholastic theology, however, was rejected by the Reformers because of "reason" flooding into theology. This influx supposedly prevented the pure Scripture from being understood. Faith was sullied over with philosophy. "The principle of 'sola scriptura' . . . sought faith in its pure, primordial form, as originally found in the Biblical Word" (#34). This biblical "Word," itself a highly sophisticated understanding, had, in this approach, no relation to the philosophic tradition of "Word," or to the "I am" of Exodus. How was "faith only" to meet this separation of faith and philosophy?

Earlier in the lecture, however, Benedict took care to explain how both in the Old and New Testaments that the theologian learned from the philosopher and the philosopher from the theologian. They learned what was ultimately implied by the "Word." This same Word was said to have been made "flesh," a Word whose meaning also requires a metaphysics to be sure it was not, as many early heresies insisted, itself an illusion. The philosophical "word" and the Word made flesh, the Word that was in the beginning, illuminated each other. Their consideration could not be separated without refusing to consider the wonderment of their similarities.

In this process, as we have seen, the Pope understands Kant to draw the logical conclusion. Faith can have no "rational" groundings. Our minds do not reveal a real world. Christ could not have been ontologically who He said He was, a Person, true God and true man in this world. Nor, in this understanding, can Scripture be addressed to real men in a real world with real minds that really understand in their own manner. The intellects of actual men are so feeble that they can only deal with "practical," not theoretical, things. This position already goes beyond Aristotle, who refused to let the admitted difference between human and the highest things cause us to cease wondering why we could know something of both. Men, it was now implied, needed only to know how to live. This latter is grounded on *sola fides*. But this "how to live" that is found in Scripture is, on this basis, not an understanding but only a supposition, an obedience without reason. Already here is an idea that will have much future to it in its working itself out. It will lead us to a world in which we can only know ourselves, but a world in which each of us have a different understanding of what we really are. We have no grounds for agreeing through some origin in nature or God.

II.

The second step in dehellenization, which followed the first step, had to do with Adolf von Harnak in the nineteenth century. Here the Pope speaks of the logical progression of principle, not merely a time sequence. He knows about Hobbes, Locke, Rousseau, and Hume. Hume's proposition that "the contrary of every matter of fact is possible" is but a more modern statement of Ibn Hazm. Granted the primacy of practical intellect as a criterion of what we should learn from Him, from His example, Jesus is no longer God. To so assume would be a theoretical thing the dimensions of which we cannot know. But Jesus is, nonetheless, a very nice man. Following Roger Bacon's rhetoric, He can inspire us to do good and avoid evil, whatever we may define these to be.

We follow Jesus, therefore, not because of who and what He is (that is, a divine Person whose meaning requires metaphysics to assist us in understanding what has been revealed to us about His being), but because of his simple "humanity." We do not "worship" or follow Christ as if He were God. Rather we imitate Him because He has good manners, because he is merely human. We do "practical" or "effective" things in imitation of this good man. "In the end, he [Christ] was presented as the father of a humanitarian moral message" (#31).

Both philosophy and systematic theology in the classical sense were out of place in this project of Harnak. Theology, he thought, has now become "historical." On a historical basis, therefore, we might be surprised to learn that theology can be "scientific" in the way modern science uses the word "scientific." Theology, once having been expelled from the university because it had no suitable object to study by scientific methods, is now back on credible terms. Theology is indeed "scientific" in the modern sense. That is, it studies what this pious man, Jesus, did on earth insofar as we have records on which to base ourselves. It is rather like studying Caesar. The primacy of "practical" reason, again that Stoic emphasis on the primacy of moral philosophy, means that what is true is what we can do, whatever it is. Our criterion of truth is an artistic, not prudential, criterion. Practical science does not judge our actions to be good or bad from principles of what we are. Rather it is a recording, as Machiavelli said, of what men "do do," whatever it is. It cannot measure what they should do as if there were some discoverable "oughtness" in nature. "Science" does not ask more than the facts, a term that itself must be understood philosophically.

Benedict recalls that he dealt with Harnak in his lecture at the University of Bonn in 1959. Following Pascal, the God of Abraham and the god of the philosophers were said to have no relation. The Pope uses this background to explain what is "new" in this second step in dehellenization. Underneath all this philosophy, Jesus was merely a man with a simple message. "Jesus was said to have put an end to worship in favour of morality" (#38). Notice here that morality is placed in opposition to worship, just the opposite relation as in classical thought where those who worship properly ought first to be moral. Jesus was a real "humanitarian." We do not "worship" man, even a fine one. The Jesus who at first was not buttressed by philosophy so that we might see his divinity, now is not divine in any sense. This is almost the opposite of what the Reformers set out to protect. The "pure" message of the gentle Jesus is inspirational, nothing more. His being does not put us in contact with the divine, but merely with the duty of inspiring one another in whatever it is we decide that is human, merely human.

In this approach, then, Jesus was not divine. No metaphysics could give us some further idea of what this divinity/humanity might mean. But because of this evaporation of metaphysical claims, Christ could now be understood by modern "reason" for the only thing he was, a good man. Previously for Harnak, this modern reason could claim no access to "faith" or "values," to use Max Weber's term. Thus we eliminate as unscientific such theological confusing elements as were implied by "Christ's divinity and the triune God." These notions had been carefully elaborated by the combination of faith and reason, but are now seen as ungrounded in any transcendence.

The "historical-critical" method, which studied only what could be known by the understanding of modern method, had the paradoxical effect, however, of allowing theology back into the university (#39). The Jesus that now comes to be studied is analyzed as a product of "practical science." Again, Harnak was interested in the university. He wanted to allow theology to re-enter it on the basis of modern "science." He thought he was saving it, dignifying it. To do this noble service, he had to narrow the definition of the kind of science theology was in itself. Jesus was back into the halls of academe not as *Logos* but as a record of what, if anything, could be established by meticulous scientific method. This method, of course, by virtue of what it conceived as its proper object, necessarily excluded the question of who and what Christ really was according to what was revealed in Scripture. In eliminating philosophy from Scripture, we ended up by eliminating the divinity from Christ.

Benedict calls this process a "self limitation of reason" (#40). He clearly implies that this self-limitation is not intrinsically or intellectually necessary. It is not itself a product of reason. This narrow approach is not the only explanation that science or reason can use in coming to terms with who Christ is or what all of reality is. The notion of the self-limitation of reason comes from Kant's Critiques (#40). Modern natural sciences, however, took this critique a step farther. It drew conclusions from its own self-limiting premises.

It is here where the issue of technology reenters the discussion. Modern science, the Pope tells us, is the result of a synthesis of "Platonism (Cartesianism) and empiricism" (#40). The "success" of technology "confirms" the fruitfulness of this approach taken in itself. He does not mean here that just any application of technology is beyond a criterion other than utility. As the Pope had earlier insisted, much that is valid is found in technology. But we need to see in what this validity consists and why. Basically, to establish this point, we must ask whether mathematics finds itself in any proper way in nature. Or is its existence an exclusive product of the mind itself in such a fashion that what it thinks mathematically is but arbitrarily applied to nature?

Initially, Benedict observes that modern science presupposes the "mathematical structure of nature." This structure implies an "intrinsic rationality" within nature, something not put there by the human mind as such. Otherwise, it would not be necessary to investigate it to see how it works, if it does. We can and do use our minds and hands to put something into effect outside of our minds, something that achieves what we want to make or do. This capacity indicates that some correspondence between what we think and what we do is found in the world. Benedict, following many things in his works, calls this background the "Platonic element of the modern understanding of nature" (#41). Plato, as we recall, was fascinated by mathematics. We should note that what is operative here is something more than a subjective imposition of mathematics by the human will on nature. The "structure" is "found" to be already there. Our minds, knowing themselves, recognize it and can use it.

Yet, following Aristotle's notion of practical intellect, of art and craft, and indeed following the notion of Genesis that man was to have "dominion" over all of nature, man can use this same nature for his own purposes. When this idea of what we want to make is finally fabricated or brought forth, truth and falsity are indicated by a "verification," whereby we repeat the exact terms of the experiment. This verification is how we find out the "truth" of our proposals (#42). The only thing that can be thus considered on this hypothesis as "scientific" is an "interplay" between mathematics and experiment. If not measured by this criterion, it is not said to be "scientific." And this restriction, Benedict thinks, is its own problem.

What follows for the university and its faculties when this "verification" criterion is used exclusively for what is called the "scientific"? "The human sciences, such as history, psychology, sociology and philosophy, attempt to conform themselves to this canon of scientificity" (#45). This application of scientific method is imposed on such disciplines, whose subject matter is not, as such, solely material. This is why the academic journals of these disciplines abound in charts, graphs, and mathematical apparatus, which rarely give real insight into the real subject matter of the discipline. They suppose that their proper subject matter is not "man" or his free activities but what is in him that can be so measured. Some things can be usefully measured, but not necessarily everything or the most important things.

This observation brings us to the same point that the Pope made about studying Jesus "scientifically." One can do so, but, by such methods, he is not studying anything more than what such methods can reveal. Harnak, in attempting to reintroduce the study of Jesus into the university, only brought in with him an exemplary man, not the Son of God, the Word, whose being requires, to be understood, more than such methods. The Jesus measured by such methods and brought into the university is not the Jesus that theology looks at and responds in reason. The method closes off the very being that is worth reasoning about.

The Pope next implicitly brings up the controverted question of "intrinsic design." "The modern concept of reason is based . . . on a synthesis between Platonism (Cartesianism) and empiricism, a synthesis confirmed by the success of technology." Notice again that the Pope approves of sensible technology. Several times in the course of the lecture, he goes out of his way to reaffirm this positive judgment. Still, we must "understand" why we approve. It is not solely just because it works.

This understanding of science and what works means we must explain "modernity" as a claim to an exclusively man-formed knowledge, something I tried to do in *At the Limits of Political Philosophy* (Ch. 3). Modernity is basically the claim, as Yves Simon says in his *A General Theory of Authority*, that the first principles of reason are themselves subject to will. Contrary to Aristotle, they do not "bind" reason to *what* is. Modernity, in its philosophic sense, means that we are bound by nothing. There is no order in things or in the mind, for that matter, that would ground any order. There is only the order we ourselves make and impose on things. This view of modernity was developed, in large part, to protect us from the notion that truth obliges us. The real question thus becomes, in the classical sense, what "limits" reason? The answer is *what is*, reality.

But the Pope continues to make the issue more specific. He sees in modernity what can be saved. Modernity "presupposes the mathematical structure of matter, its intrinsic rationality, which makes it possible to understand how matter works and use it efficiently: this basic premise is . . . the Platonic element in the modern understanding of nature" (#41). We might also recall that the medieval idea of the *quadrivium*, which everyone had to study in the university, was, following Plato, based on the study of arithmetic, geometry, music, and astronomy. What differentiated these disciplinary studies was in effect the Pope's point. Arithmetic studies numbers in themselves, geometry studied number in space, music studied it in time, and astronomy studied it in both space and time. The study of the *Republic* shows the central place of numbers in the educative formation of our minds. Yet, we still need to confront the metaphysical problem of what is the relation of a reality that displays order and its source? This is an issue that this lecture does not hesitate to confront.

This same science, following Bacon, but also Genesis, refers to the fact that we can use this nature and its order for "our purposes." We can verify and falsify our attempts to understand nature or make something out of it. What is normally meant today by science is this restricted "interplay of mathematical and empirical elements" (#45). This interplay is good as far as it goes. But this method, "by its very nature," excludes God and makes efforts to understand His presence to be considered "unscientific" because this one method is the only one permitted. It restricts itself to quantified objects (#46).

What do we do about this situation? First, if we maintain that "theology" must be "scientific," not in Aquinas's sense, but after the manner of modern physical sciences in order to be respectable in the university, then we reduce what the whole scope of reason is to the terms of mathematical inquiry (#46). But God is not a big number, however much God is *Logos*. Not only does this method reduce God to a number, but it reduces man to the same status. In losing God we lose man, something John Paul II pointed out again and again. "The specifically human questions about our origin and destiny, the questions raised by religion and ethics, then have no place within the purview of collective reason as defined by 'science' and thus must be relegated to the realm of the subjective" (#48). This means that such basic questions can no longer be asked in a spirit of "reason." It also implies that the spiritual knowledge acquired by other means in other cultures are considered worthless and from which nothing important can be learned. In other words, the Regensburg Lecture is also a defense of the rational statues of genuine religious knowledge.

What follows from this rejection of reason in its broader sense? Logically, what follows is "cultural pluralism," the third "dehellenization." Strauss and Voegelin both made the same point about "historicism," the claim that truth also changes with time. Everyone, every culture, or every era comes up with its own "truth." No objectively definable difference can be established between what the cannibals do and what the saints do. Specifically human questions are arbitrarily defined as "subjective," with no objective referent. "The subject then decides, on the basis of his experiences, what he considers tenable in matters of religion" (#48). What follows from this premise? The sole criterion of what is "ethical" is the "subjective conscience," which has no way of agreeing on some standard measure of right and wrong. As an American Supreme Court decision once had it, everyone decides his own truth or worldview.

If there is no standard but subjective conscience, then there can be no "common good," the central theme of classical social and political thought that follows a realist understanding of what man is (#49). A common good is the recognition of many objective goods worth bringing into effect. Everyone can see the reasonableness of the goods that are brought into being or affirmed in being. It does not take an act of faith to see the good, as it does when the only criterion of good is subjective conscience. Benedict frankly acknowledges that this subjective understanding of our good is "a dangerous state of affairs for humanity."

Indeed, the Pope sees it is at the origin of what he calls dangerous "pathologies of religion and reason." I would take this pathology to mean that the pursuit of subjective good, as it has no objective limit, can take up extreme causes as if they were themselves the real human good. Deviant goods command the same enthusiasm and energy as real goods. The origins of political aberrations are thus rooted in a theory of subjectivism, not merely in occasional mental disorder. Neither evolution, sociology, nor psychology thus provides an adequate basis for a common good (#49).

With this background, the Pope again formulates the third "dehellenization," which he states "is now in progress" (#50). Before he reaches his final conclusion to this lecture, however, this third state needs explication. Everyone is aware of the missionary efforts of the Church all through modernity beginning with medieval Franciscan missionaries across Asia, Jesuits in China, many orders in India, south Asia, and Africa. The Church itself looked very "multi-cultural." Did the Church not herself do exactly what the Pope criticized?

When the Church, however, sought to "inculturate" itself into other cultures, it did so on the basis of at least something that all cultures either had or should have had in common, namely, reason (#51). This reason is what was learned from Greek philosophy, though it was not simply identified with Greece. Indeed, while it presupposed Rome's own absorption of Greek culture, this confrontation of the Bible and Greek philosophy was the first multi-cultural effort, the hellenization of the Christian understanding of itself. On this basis, it could address itself to reason in intelligible terms. We do not want to go "behind" this effort as if somehow this endeavor were not itself part of the initial dynamism of the faith with regard to what it was about. Benedict's point is that, as a strategy for modern missionary methods, the proposal to "get behind" the hellenization of the early Church and approach other cultures without reason is a wrong turn (#51). Either the un-Christianized culture will itself have elements of the same reason that philosophy knows, or it will have, as a cultural basis, un-philosophical positions that need to be reordered in reason.

Obviously, each culture may do what we do by genuflecting differently or wearing different kinds of dress (#53). But "the fundamental decisions made about the relationship between faith and the use of human reason is part of the faith itself; they are developments consonant with the nature of faith itself" (#53). Faith is addressed to a reason that has asked the basic philosophic questions of itself and not found complete or satisfactory answers. This multicultural third "dehellenization" implied that those cultures that do not have a tradition of reason need not examine themselves about their own theoretic and rational premises. The classic notion of Christian "mission," however, always included, or should have included, this element of reason. It is not to be assumed that cultures with elements of un-reason in their culture would necessarily welcome a critique of their own customs or practices. Both the tradition of reason and faith can be dangerous. The facing of this danger seems to be what the missionary impulse is about, that revelation's own inner dynamism is not content with what is disordered.

The Christian faith proposed itself to other cultures not as a conquest but as understanding of what was good in a culture, but also of what was unreasonable. What was unreasonable was against the true human good and ultimately against the possibility of faith. Agonizing controversies, thus, were pondered over whether having ten wives was "cultural" or "unreasonable." Distinctions had to be made. But Benedict's point here is that because of the relation of Greek reason and faith, a basis already existed for an approach to any other culture, even an "un-reasonable"

one. "The fundamental decisions made about the relationship between faith and the use of human reason are part of
the faith itself; they are developments consonant with the
nature of the faith itself" (#53). The effort to get behind
the hellenization of Christianity to a pure form without
this presumed burden of reason is itself contrary to the
workings of the faith in its initial and formative period. To
arrive at a faith that was not oriented to reason as such was
itself not what the faith taught of itself about what it must
do.

Chapter V.

REVELATION AND CULTURE

"Here I am reminded of something Socrates said to Phaedo. In their earlier conversation, many false philosophical opinions had been raised, and so Socrates says: 'It would be easily understandable if someone became so annoyed at all these false notions that for the rest of his life he despised and mocked all talk about being – but in this way he would be deprived of the truth of existence and would suffer a great loss" (#61).

In his conclusion, Benedict again remarks that he is not interested in "putting the clock back to the time before the Enlightenment." This is a remark that may well illuminate Strauss's ideas about the need to return to the classics to find what has gone wrong with our modern mind (#54). What we find in Strauss is reason plus some Hebrew revelation. But we do not find what we find here, namely, Christian revelation with its own claims on reason. This difference is fair enough. Both traditions find something reasonable in the Old Testament.

But the Pope has argued a consequence of the historicist position by using Strauss's words that cannibalism is merely a matter of taste. In a hint of "intrinsic design," he adds, "the scientific ethics, moreover, is the will to be obedient to the truth, and, as such, it embodies the attitude which reflects one of the basic tenets of Christianity" (#55). Thus, for all his problems with the formulations of "modern science," Benedict sees within its stated ethos a claim that it seeks the truth of things. Needless to say, this is what revelation is about and what classical philosophy was about. Benedict has, in principle, broached the question of a possible theoretic reconciliation with science and science with a faith directed to reason

Benedict indicates that consequences of the limitation of the use of reason, its reductionism to a certain method, is, in the more complete sense, described in *Fides et Ratio*. This limit, in a carefully selected phrase, is said to be "self-imposed" by the scientists themselves (#56). That is, it is not itself a requirement of reason as such. Rather it is a "requirement" of a reason determined to close itself off from certain presumably unwelcome conclusions, namely, the possibility that science is not opposed to faith but aided and completed by it. More than one method exists in philosophy. Things that are not "mathematical," – *what is* – including ourselves and our minds, really are known.

Theology thus belongs to the university, as does metaphysics, because both use reason to address themselves to questions that are real. These approaches are not currently permitted to be explored by any other method but "scientific," in the restricted or reductionist use of that term (#57). Again we see that this lecture is in fact addressed to the theoretic question of "what is a university," or to use Newman's famous phrase, to "the idea of a university." Theology is not merely a "historical" discipline, in the Harnak sense of only knowing what is to be examined by sciences with a mathematical basis. Why theology is properly in the university is because of "the rationality of faith" (#57). That is, it explains the basic meaning of revelation and expounds reasons for it or reasons against its own truth. This means that theology both has a basis in reason, entitling it to be in the university with its own method, but also a reason not to be excluded on the basis of a limited "scientific method," a method that itself can be examined in reason.

The "positivist" reason, to which Strauss and Voegelin also referred, cannot enter into "dialogue" with other cultures that are concerned with the meaning of God and man (#58). Thus, the Pope's concern with Islam, though he does not explicitly state this, is also his concern with India, China, and other cultures on the same basis. That is, these cultures have their own rationale for what they do, but this rationale itself is to be examined by the universal culture of reason. This examination is not an "imposition" of Greek or Christian mind on other cultures. Rather it is a reasoned examination of what, in any culture, is held in the precise terms of its reasonableness. One must add, any claim to "another kind of reason" is itself subject to this same process. No such claim can claim reason as if it has other standards or principles closed to reason which reason cannot at least examine. This process does not place "reason" over faith, but rather addresses any claim to intelligibility in terms of reason.

More immediately, this attention to culture and reason is also a concern with our own Western mind that, in multiculturalism and in positivism, has denied reason its rightful place, even its rightful understanding. Multiculturalism, as a philosophic principle, is, logically, but another way of saying that "cannibalism is all right," merely a matter of "taste." Why not? But if not, give reasons. We all know what happens, for example, to many bodies of aborted fetuses, used for cosmetics or used parts. They are, it is said, used to promote the good of others or defined subjectively as non-human. The sort of culture in which such claims are offered makes cannibalism look positively rational. Islam, on this score, to give it credit, is not so irrational as many in the West are when it comes to such matters though Islam's practices of marriage and family cannot avoid their own examination in reason.

At this point, Benedict returns to the question of science and particularly its mathematical foundation in quantity. He frankly acknowledges that he "attempts to show" the point he is trying to make. Is "positivist reason" the only reason in the field? It is quite clear that there is a general decline of "continental" philosophy even on the continent of Europe. It is being replaced even there by positivist science. However, the "Platonic element" that founded Western thinking is itself mathematically oriented.

"Modern scientific reason with its intrinsically Platonic element bears within itself a question which points beyond itself and beyond the possibilities of its methodology" (#59). Notice that the words used are "points beyond itself" and "beyond the possibilities of its methodology." Both of these "pointings" indicate that, in spite of its own professed self-understanding, science is not, even within itself, a closed system having only the human mind at its origins.

Benedict continues, rather bluntly, "modern scientific reason quite simply has to accept the rational structure of matter and the correspondence between our spirit and the prevailing rational structures of nature as a given, on which its methodology has to be based" (#59). The fact is that something is already in quantified nature that is not put there by human intelligence. Yet this same intelligence can grasp it and refine what it means in a mathematical formula or system.[1] Why do things work? Because what we know in some sense is already present in that on which we work for our own purposes. Not everything is "imposed" by our

1. In his Verona address of October 19, 2006, Benedict returned to this subject of mathematics: "Mathematics, as such, is a creation of our intelligence: the correspondence between its structures and the real structures of the universe – which is the presupposition of all modern scientific and technological developments, already expressly formulated by Galileo Galilei with the famous affirmation that the book of nature is written in mathematical language – arouses our admiration and raises a big question. It implies, in fact, that the universe itself is structured in an intelligent manner, such that a profound correspondence exists between our subjective reason and the objective reason in nature. It then becomes inevitable to ask one-self if there might not be a single original intelligence that is the common font of them both." *L'Osservatore Romano, English*, October 25, 2006, 8.

minds. Nor can everything out there be ignored or in some Kantian sense declared unknowable.

But Benedict is not yet finished with this line of reasoning. He knows when scientific answers are not complete in their own order. Their formulation does raise more questions yet to be addressed. Benedict frankly tells us that there is yet a "real question" to be faced. What is this "real question?" This question cannot be answered by science itself but has to be "remanded by the natural sciences to other modes and planes of thought – to philosophy and theology." Aristotle had remarked at the beginning of the *Ethics* that we should not expect more certitude of a science than its subject matter allowed. Because something is not capable of being responded to by the method of science, because of its own object, it does not follow that reason cannot take a look at the matter from other angles and principles. The closing off of academic or scientific discussion to one method itself based on mathematics and its object does not mean that everything is closed and nothing further remains to be considered. The meaning of philosophy is to address reason to the whole, including to those questions not capable of response by a science perfectly competent in its own order.

The traditions of other cultures and other disciplines do have something to say to us. We can address our minds to their scope and meaning. The way scientific method has worked out, instead of honestly facing the implications of these other modes, it has simply left them unexamined.[2]

2   Probably the best, briefest, and most insightful book to illustrate this

We can in fact listen to "the great experiences and insights of the religious traditions of humanity, and those of the Christian faith in particular" (#61). We have to learn that listening is itself an experience, a testimony about reality. What men have said and experienced is "too a source of knowledge."[3] To ignore or deny such real and direct knowledge, Benedict adds, "would be an unacceptable restriction of our listening and responding" (#61). What is again worth noting here is the constant theme in this lecture of the deliberate self-restriction and reduction of knowledge so that essential elements of our real experience have no place in our picture of the world.

At this point, the Pope turns aside a bit to wonder about what is the reason for this deliberate restriction on one's own mind. One cannot help but be delighted to see that he explains his point by recalling Socrates in the *Phaedo*. This passage is mindful of Aristotle's discussion in chapter seven of the *Ethics*. Here Aristotle explains how is it intellectually possible to explain both how and why we err. He explains how and why we are responsible when we do so err.

Benedict recalls that in this dialogue, many "false philosophical opinions" had been discussed among those

point, in terms mindful of Benedict's very analysis, is E. F. Schumacher, *A Guide for the Perplexed* (New York: Harper Colophon, 1977).

3   Jean Daniélou's little book, *La crise actuelle de l'intelligence* (Paris: Apostolat des Editions, 1969), contains a very succinct and similar approach to that of the Holy Father here by emphasizing the kind of knowledge that we acquire in friendship, conversation, love, and generosity.

present. This is the dialogue that takes place on Socrates' last day. What he does on his last day, as his good wife Xanthippe said, is to do what he did every day. He spent his time discussing the highest things with his young friends, the potential philosophers. They are annoyed at Socrates for accepting so calmly the death sentence he had received at the trial. They did not think it was at all just. Simmias and Cebes, in particular, two young Thebans, had inquired about the immortality of the soul, the reason Socrates seemed to be so calm. Socrates had patiently examined each of their objections. They finally had to admit that his reasonings, contrary to what they might want, were coherent and correct.

It is here that Benedict cites Socrates – remember that John Paul II cited Socrates' trial at least twice as itself something that prefigured the death of Christ. But Benedict is concerned with another issue, namely, why do people choose not to see the truth? It is a subtle point. Nor is it surprising that Socrates has already faced the issue. This is what Socrates says, "it would be easily understandable if someone became so annoyed at all these false notions that for the rest of his life he despised and mocked all talk about being – but in this way he would be deprived of the truth of existence and would suffer a great loss" (#61, 90c–d). What does this passage say?

First, a multiplicity of false notions can very well discourage us from pursuing the truth. Is there such a multiplicity? Of course. Should we let this variety of false propositions govern us? By no means. Why? Because, in so doing, we would be "deprived of the truth of existence." The "truth of existence" is the heart of what we want to know. We can suffer great mental losses because of what we refuse to pursue, even midst the difficulties.

Why do we refuse to pursue this "truth of existence?" The only answer we can discover is because we do not want to find it if, as we suspect it might, it goes contrary to our expectations, to what we want to do or how we choose to live. We would not want to know the coherence of things if it requires us to change our ways or our understanding of things, or especially our relation to God. But the Pope is right. A "great loss" ensues if we refuse to pursue the truth wherever it is found. This "great loss" is delineated by the terms of this Regensburg Lecture, that faith and reason are not presented against science as such.

The Pope states the issue clearly. The whole of civilization is at stake. It is at stake because of what we hold in our minds and follow with our wills. This issue goes to the core of the supposed conflict between science and faith: "The West had long been endangered by this aversion to the questions which underlie its rationality, and can only suffer great harm thereby. The courage to engage the whole breadth of reason, and not the denial of its grandeur – this is the programme with which a theology grounded in Biblical faith enters into the debate of our time" (#62). The West is endangered because of its mind, because of its failure to comprehend *what* is. What does overturn the suppositions that "underlie" our rationality? Obviously, it can only be the denial of rationality itself in all its dimensions.

It is the denial of reason in the name of reason, the "self-limitation" of reason so that it does not confront what is within its full scope. There is, I suspect, on a larger scale, a fear that the truth exists and that it is in fact truth.

The virtue of courage, which the Holy Father mentions, is normally considered to be the military virtue, the virtue of the preservation of existence itself. Here it has other connotations. We need courage even to "engage in the whole breadth of reason." We need courage not to "deny its grandeur." It is at this point that Benedict maintains that "a theology grounded in Biblical faith" can enter into "the debate of our time." In his encyclical, *Deus Caritas Est*, Benedict made the following remark: "By their own inner logic, these initial, somewhat philosophical reflections on the essence of love have now brought us to the threshold of biblical faith" (#7). This "inner logic" is not arbitrary. Reason by being itself comes to the "threshold" of faith. There is no appeal to a faith in spite of reason in any fundamental sense.

What is this debate? It is the debate about the place of theology in issues of reason. Faith has its own intelligibility, but it is not an intelligibility opposed to reason. It is an intelligibility that fosters reason to be more reason. It too is addressed to reason and formulated, because of the encounter with the Greek mind, in terms that are said to be open to reason. This approach does not claim that human reason is divine reason, but still it is reason. Contrary perhaps to Aristotle's distance between the First Mover and the human intellect, the human intellect remains intellect whose perfection in grace is able to be destined to the divine intellect.

> The faith of the Church has always insisted that between God and us, between his eternal Creator Spirit and our created reason there exists a real analogy, in which . . . unlikeness remains infinitely greater than likeness, yet not to the point of abolishing analogy and its language. God does not become more divine when we push him away from us in a sheer impenetrable voluntarism; rather, the truly divine God is the God who has revealed himself as *logos* and, as *logos*, has acted and continues to act lovingly on our behalf (#27).

This immensely important passage is literally the charter by which we are to defend both the transcendence of God and His ability to communicate what He wishes to us in such a manner that we can both understand it and see that it is true because we have the powers to do so. Thus as the Pope's first Encyclical might be called "Deus est *agape*," so this lecture is "Deus est *logos*."

The one thing that Benedict does not touch on in this lecture is the condition of theology itself, a theology that neglects reason, something that *Fides et Ratio* admonished. The Regensburg Lecture, in addressing itself to science, also addresses itself to that theory of university associated with Harnak, which would welcome theology into the university only because its limits were themselves defined by the modern scientific method. Thus, in seeking to save science and philosophy, Benedict also seeks to save theology precisely because of the initial encounter of Scripture and the Greek mind. biblical faith, then, is not an alien presence in the "debates of our time." Its absence is precisely what causes these same debates to wander off into alternative ideologies and myths that cannot account for *all that is*. The alternative to an "impenetrable voluntarism" is a faith addressed to reason and a reason based in *what is*.

CONCLUSION

Benedict concludes the Regensburg Lecture by repeating precisely what Manuel II, the much-maligned Byzantine emperor under siege from Islam before his city, told the learned Persian gentleman: "Not to act reasonably (with *logos*) is contrary to the nature of God" (#63). Clearly, the purpose of this lecture is to state why this proposition, no matter who said it, is true, all times, all places, all cultures. One cannot be "reasonable" and avoid the implications of this argument. To affirm the opposite is to affirm a contradiction of mind and reality. Not to act reasonably is not merely contrary to the nature of man, but contrary to the nature of God. The Pope is deadly serious here. No single idea is more dangerous to our kind than the idea that God approves violence in His name. To claim to do violence, that is, to take the lives of the innocent, in the name of God is precisely blasphemy.

But the claim that acting "unreasonably" is according to the nature of God is not merely blasphemous. By the same logic, it is in practice destructive of any human good and order. This claim to act reasonably in acting violently is the one "irrationality" that, in the name of reason, must be stopped, not merely in the mind but in the streets. And, following Aristotle, to prevent an irrational act against the innocent may, with proper prudence, itself be rational, may be required in the name of reason. The preventing of unreason is not itself unreason. The refusal to stop irrational acts, however, and to so refuse in the name of reason is itself unreasonable. Coercion exists in law and politics to cover this necessity when it occurs, as it does in the history and daily lives of our kind.

What is to be remarked is that apparently no one in the German audience in Regensburg saw any reason to take to the streets or protest because of what was said there. One cannot suppose that everyone in that audience agreed with what was presented for consideration. The Pope's amusing introduction to his lecture recalled a skeptical colleague at the University of Bonn. The man quipped that the existence of the two theology faculties there was odd because they both, as far as he could see by his philosophy, dealt with "nothing," namely, with God (#6). No one wanted to attack or intimidate this academic skeptic because of his view. Nor did the skeptic professor, in his turn, argue that therefore theology should not be in the university if it addressed itself to reason. Theologians can also think. Skepticism has its own intellectual problems.

Yet, I do sometimes wonder, at how many universities in the world is there really freedom to give a lecture such as the one the Professor Pope presented at Regensburg? True, John Paul II always gave a learned and moving lecture at a university in every place he visited. But today in the West, such freedom is rare. Lectures, especially those about the truth of Christianity and what it holds, even in Catholic universities, are greeted with claims that they violate "multiculturalism" or "toleration" or "freedom."

Yet, Benedict – "Benedict the Brave," as the *Wall Street Journal* rightly called him – also had immediately in mind the intimidation that appears after attempts to understand or even playfully tease Islam, as in the Danish-cartoon case. Efforts or threats that forbid any discussion must stop. This is but a first step. Islamic peoples who abide in this reaction are their own worst enemies. They reveal that they are the problem by their own actions. The internet is filled with pleas to Muslim thinkers and people to "speak out" against the "terrorists." The Pope's lecture perhaps indicates why they, in large measure, do not. Many do not protest because they do not see anything wrong with it. To engage the rationality of this latter view is what must follow once violence itself is prevented.

The notion that we can create our own positive law and do "what is right" by simply doing what the positive law says – clearly, abortion is also irrational violence against the innocent – must also stop. It is not true that the civil order, à la Hobbes, is safe if we just forbid the asking of the deepest questions of reason, including its own validity. At the deepest levels, what we hold is what makes the public order to be unsafe. Ideas, good and bad, do not always come forth into action. When violent action is a product of thought, it is time to examine the thought. This examination was the function of the Regensburg Lecture.

Wars are not caused by arms and we, including religious people, should stop saying they are. They are ultimately caused by persons with ideas, wrong ideas. The Pope was right to call our attention, intellectually, to just why certain well-articulated ideas are a problem. The first step in stopping violence is to understand what *logos,* in all its dimensions, implies in all cultures, not just Islam. Mind is universal, as Cicero often said. The Pope, in this basic sense, was repeating, via a Byzantine Roman Emperor, this great Roman philosopher who himself carefully read the thinkers of Greece and even sent his son to study there. "' Not to act reasonably, not to act with *logos,* is contrary to the nature of God,' said Manuel II, according to his Christian understanding of God, in response to his Persian interlocutor. It is to this great *logos,* to this breadth of reason, that we invite our partners in the dialogue of cultures. To rediscover it constantly is the great task of the university" (#63). These final words of the Regensburg Lecture are spare.

The principle at issue is clear even if spoken by an Emperor to a Persian gentleman and recalled by a Pope. What is being invited is a "dialogue of cultures." Can anything in reason be said against this principle that would justify its denial and leave the freedom to do the opposite of what it concludes? If no alternative can be sustained in reason, then the groundwork for a whole new relationship of Christianity and Islam, of all cultures, of the West's own self-understanding, can be laid. Finally, to repeat what we said in the beginning, "the task of the university" is nothing less than the constant, not discovery, for it has already been discovered, but the *rediscovery* of reason. In the end, ultimate things have to be rediscovered in each of our own souls. They are not passed on without our free consent to their truth. It is on this basis that civilization exists.

Appendix I

THE REGENSURG LECTURE

Apostolic Journey of His Holiness Benedict XVI
to München, Altötting and Regensberg
(September 9–14, 2006)

Meeting with the Representatives of Science

Lecture of the Holy Father

Aula Magna of the University of Regensburg
Tuesday, 12 September 2006

Faith, Reason and the University
*Memories and Reflections**

#1) *Your Eminences, Your Magnificences, Your Excellencies,*
Distinguished Ladies and Gentlemen,

#2) It is a moving experience for me to be back again in the
university and to be able once again to give a lecture at this
podium. I think back to those years when, after a pleasant
period at the Freisinger Hochschule, I began teaching at
the University of Bonn. That was in 1959, in the days of
the old university made up of ordinary professors.

#3) The various chairs had neither assistants nor secretaries, but in recompense there was much direct contact with students and in particular among the professors themselves. We would meet before and after lessons in the rooms of the teaching staff. There was a lively exchange with historians, philosophers, philologists and, naturally, between the two theological faculties.

#4) Once a semester there was a *dies academicus*, when professors from every faculty appeared before the students of the entire university, making possible a genuine experience of *universitas* – something that you too, Magnificent Rector, just mentioned – the experience, in other words, of the fact that despite our specializations which at times make it difficult to communicate with each other, we made up a whole, working in everything on the basis of a single rationality with its various aspects and sharing responsibility for the right use of reason – this reality became a lived experience.

#5) The university was also very proud of its two theological faculties. It was clear that, by inquiring about the reasonableness of faith, they too carried out a work which is necessarily part of the "whole" of the *universitas scientiarum*, even if not everyone could share the faith which theologians seek to correlate with reason as a whole.

#6) This profound sense of coherence within the universe of reason was not troubled, even when it was once reported that a colleague had said there was something odd about our university: it had two faculties devoted to something that did not exist: God.

#7) That even in the face of such radical scepticism it is still necessary and reasonable to raise the question of God through the use of reason, and to do so in the context of the tradition of the Christian faith: this, within the university as a whole, was accepted without question.

#8) I was reminded of all this recently, when I read the edition by Professor Theodore Khoury (Münster) of part of the dialogue carried on – perhaps in 1391 in the winter barracks near Ankara – by the erudite Byzantine emperor Manuel II Paleologus and an educated Persian on the subject of Christianity and Islam, and the truth of both.[1] It was presumably the emperor himself who set down this dialogue, during the siege of Constantinople between 1394 and 1402; and this would explain why his arguments are given in greater detail than those of his Persian interlocutor.[2]

#9) The dialogue ranges widely over the structures of faith contained in the Bible and in the Qur'an, and deals especially with the image of God and of man, while necessarily returning repeatedly to the relationship between – as they were called – three "Laws" or "rules of life": the Old Testament, the New Testament and the Qur'an.

#10) It is not my intention to discuss this question in the present lecture; here I would like to discuss only one point

– itself rather marginal to the dialogue as a whole – which, in the context of the issue of "faith and reason", I found interesting and which can serve as the starting-point for my reflections on this issue.

#11) In the seventh conversation (διάλεξις – controversy) edited by Professor Khoury, the emperor touches on the theme of the holy war. The emperor must have known that surah 2, 256 reads: "There is no compulsion in religion". According to some of the experts, this is probably one of the suras of the early period, when Mohammed was still powerless and under threat.

#12) But naturally the emperor also knew the instructions, developed later and recorded in the Qur'an, concerning holy war. Without descending to details, such as the difference in treatment accorded to those who have the "Book" and the "infidels", he addresses his interlocutor with a startling brusqueness, a brusqueness that we find unacceptable, on the central question about the relationship between religion and violence in general, saying: "Show me just what Mohammed brought that was new, and there you will find things only evil and inhuman, such as his command to spread by the sword the faith he preached."[3]

#13) The emperor, after having expressed himself so forcefully, goes on to explain in detail the reasons why spreading the faith through violence is something unreasonable. Violence is incompatible with the nature of God and the nature of the soul. "God", he says, "is not pleased by blood

– and not acting reasonably (σὺν λόγῳ) is contrary to God's nature. Faith is born of the soul, not the body. Whoever would lead someone to faith needs the ability to speak well and to reason properly, without violence and threats. . . . To convince a reasonable soul, one does not need a strong arm, or weapons of any kind, or any other means of threatening a person with death. . . ."[4]

#14) The decisive statement in this argument against violent conversion is this: not to act in accordance with reason is contrary to God's nature.[5] The editor, Theodore Khoury, observes: For the emperor, as a Byzantine shaped by Greek philosophy, this statement is self-evident. But for Muslim teaching, God is absolutely transcendent. His will is not bound up with any of our categories, even that of rationality.[6]

#15) Here Khoury quotes a work of the noted French Islamist R. Arnaldez, who points out that Ibn Hazm went so far as to state that God is not bound even by his own word, and that nothing would oblige him to reveal the truth to us. Were it God's will, we would even have to practise idolatry.[7]

#16) At this point, as far as understanding of God and thus the concrete practice of religion is concerned, we are faced with an unavoidable dilemma. Is the conviction that acting unreasonably contradicts God's nature merely a Greek idea, or is it always and intrinsically true?

#17) I believe that here we can see the profound harmony

between what is Greek in the best sense of the word and the Biblical understanding of faith in God. Modifying the first verse of the Book of Genesis, the first verse of the whole Bible, John began the prologue of his Gospel with the words: "In the beginning was the λόγος". This is the very word used by the emperor: God acts, σὺ λόγω, with *logos*. *Logos* means both reason and word – a reason which is creative and capable of self-communication, precisely as reason.

#18) John thus spoke the final word on the Biblical concept of God, and in this word all the often toilsome and tortuous threads of Biblical faith find their culmination and synthesis. In the beginning was the *logos*, and the *logos* is God, says the Evangelist.

#19) The encounter between the Biblical message and Greek thought did not happen by chance. The vision of Saint Paul, who saw the roads to Asia barred and in a dream saw a Macedonian man plead with him: "Come over to Macedonia and help us!" (cf. *Acts* 16:6–10) – this vision can be interpreted as a "distillation" of the intrinsic necessity of a rapprochement between Biblical faith and Greek inquiry.

#20) In point of fact, this rapprochement had been going on for some time. The mysterious name of God, revealed from the burning bush, a name which separates this God from all other divinities with their many names and simply asserts being, "I am", already presents a challenge to the notion of myth, to which Socrates' attempt to vanquish and transcend myth stands in close analogy.[8]

#21) Within the Old Testament, the process which started at the burning bush came to new maturity at the time of the Exile, when the God of Israel, an Israel now deprived of its land and worship, was proclaimed as the God of heaven and earth and described in a simple formula which echoes the words uttered at the burning bush: "I am". This new understanding of God is accompanied by a kind of enlightenment, which finds stark expression in the mockery of gods who are merely the work of human hands (cf. *Ps* 115).

#22) Thus, despite the bitter conflict with those Hellenistic rulers who sought to accommodate it forcibly to the customs and idolatrous cult of the Greeks, Biblical faith, in the Hellenistic period, encountered the best of Greek thought at a deep level, resulting in a mutual enrichment evident especially in the later wisdom literature.

#23) Today we know that the Greek translation of the Old Testament produced at Alexandria – the Septuagint – is more than a simple (and in that sense really less than satisfactory) translation of the Hebrew text: it is an independent textual witness and a distinct and important step in the history of revelation, one which brought about this encounter in a way that was decisive for the birth and spread of Christianity.[9]

#24) A profound encounter of faith and reason is taking place here, an encounter between genuine enlightenment and religion. From the very heart of Christian faith and, at the same time, the heart of Greek thought now joined to faith, Manuel II was able to say: Not to act "with *logos*" is contrary to God's nature.

#25) In all honesty, one must observe that in the late Middle Ages we find trends in theology which would sunder this synthesis between the Greek spirit and the Christian spirit. In contrast with the so-called intellectualism of Augustine and Thomas, there arose with Duns Scotus a voluntarism which, in its later developments, led to the claim that we can only know God's *voluntas ordinata*. Beyond this is the realm of God's freedom, in virtue of which he could have done the opposite of everything he has actually done.

#26) This gives rise to positions which clearly approach those of Ibn Hazm and might even lead to the image of a capricious God, who is not even bound to truth and goodness. God's transcendence and otherness are so exalted that our reason, our sense of the true and good, are no longer an authentic mirror of God, whose deepest possibilities remain eternally unattainable and hidden behind his actual decisions.

#27) As opposed to this, the faith of the Church has always insisted that between God and us, between his eternal

Creator Spirit and our created reason there exists a real analogy, in which – as the Fourth Lateran Council in 1215 stated – unlikeness remains infinitely greater than likeness, yet not to the point of abolishing analogy and its language. God does not become more divine when we push him away from us in a sheer, impenetrable voluntarism; rather, the truly divine God is the God who has revealed himself as *logos* and, as *logos*, has acted and continues to act lovingly on our behalf. Certainly, love, as Saint Paul says, "transcends" knowledge and is thereby capable of perceiving more than thought alone (cf. *Eph* 3:19); nonetheless it continues to be love of the God who is *Logos*.

#28) Consequently, Christian worship is, again to quote Paul – "λογικη λατρεία", worship in harmony with the eternal Word and with our reason (cf. *Rom* 12:1).[10]

#29) This inner rapprochement between Biblical faith and Greek philosophical inquiry was an event of decisive importance not only from the standpoint of the history of religions, but also from that of world history – it is an event which concerns us even today. Given this convergence, it is not surprising that Christianity, despite its origins and some significant developments in the East, finally took on its historically decisive character in Europe.

#30) We can also express this the other way around: this convergence, with the subsequent addition of the Roman heritage, created Europe and remains the foundation of what can rightly be called Europe.

#31) The thesis that the critically purified Greek heritage forms an integral part of Christian faith has been countered by the call for a dehellenization of Christianity – a call which has more and more dominated theological discussions since the beginning of the modern age. Viewed more closely, three stages can be observed in the programme of dehellenization: although interconnected, they are clearly distinct from one another in their motivations and objectives.[11]

#32) Dehellenization first emerges in connection with the postulates of the Reformation in the sixteenth century.

#33) Looking at the tradition of scholastic theology, the Reformers thought they were confronted with a faith system totally conditioned by philosophy, that is to say an articulation of the faith based on an alien system of thought. As a result, faith no longer appeared as a living historical Word but as one element of an overarching philosophical system.

#34) The principle of *sola scriptura*, on the other hand, sought faith in its pure, primordial form, as originally found in the Biblical Word. Metaphysics appeared as a premise derived from another source, from which faith had to be liberated in order to become once more fully itself.

#35) When Kant stated that he needed to set thinking aside in order to make room for faith, he carried this programme forward with a radicalism that the Reformers could never have foreseen. He thus anchored faith exclusively in practical reason, denying it access to reality as a whole.

#36) The liberal theology of the nineteenth and twentieth centuries ushered in a second stage in the process of dehellenization, with Adolf von Harnack as its outstanding representative.

#37) When I was a student, and in the early years of my teaching, this programme was highly influential in Catholic theology too. It took as its point of departure Pascal's distinction between the God of the philosophers and the God of Abraham, Isaac and Jacob. In my inaugural lecture at Bonn in 1959, I tried to address the issue,[12] and I do not intend to repeat here what I said on that occasion, but I would like to describe at least briefly what was new about this second stage of dehellenization.

#38) Harnack's central idea was to return simply to the man Jesus and to his simple message, underneath the accretions of theology and indeed of hellenization: this simple message was seen as the culmination of the religious development of humanity. Jesus was said to have put an end to worship in favour of morality. In the end he was presented as the father of a humanitarian moral message.

#39) Fundamentally, Harnack's goal was to bring Christianity back into harmony with modern reason, liberating it, that is to say, from seemingly philosophical and theological elements, such as faith in Christ's divinity and the triune God. In this sense, historical-critical exegesis of the New Testament, as he saw it, restored to theology its place within the university: theology, for Harnack, is something essentially historical and therefore strictly scientific. What it is able to say critically about Jesus is, so to speak, an expression of practical reason and consequently it can take its rightful place within the university.

#40) Behind this thinking lies the modern self-limitation of reason, classically expressed in Kant's "Critiques", but in the meantime further radicalized by the impact of the natural sciences. This modern concept of reason is based, to put it briefly, on a synthesis between Platonism (Cartesianism) and empiricism, a synthesis confirmed by the success of technology.

#41) On the one hand it presupposes the mathematical structure of matter, its intrinsic rationality, which makes it possible to understand how matter works and use it efficiently: this basic premise is, so to speak, the Platonic element in the modern understanding of nature.

#42) On the other hand, there is nature's capacity to be exploited for our purposes, and here only the possibility of verification or falsification through experimentation can yield decisive certainty.

#43) The weight between the two poles can, depending on the circumstances, shift from one side to the other. As strongly positivistic a thinker as J. Monod has declared himself a convinced Platonist/Cartesian.

#44) This gives rise to two principles which are crucial for the issue we have raised.

#45) First, only the kind of certainty resulting from the interplay of mathematical and empirical elements can be considered scientific. Anything that would claim to be science must be measured against this criterion. Hence the human sciences, such as history, psychology, sociology and philosophy, attempt to conform themselves to this canon of scientificity.

#46) A second point, which is important for our reflections, is that by its very nature this method excludes the question of God, making it appear an unscientific or pre-scientific question. Consequently, we are faced with a reduction of the radius of science and reason, one which needs to be questioned.

#47) I will return to this problem later. In the meantime, it must be observed that from this standpoint any attempt to maintain theology's claim to be "scientific" would end up reducing Christianity to a mere fragment of its former self.

#48) But we must say more: if science as a whole is this and this alone, then it is man himself who ends up being reduced, for the specifically human questions about our origin and destiny, the questions raised by religion and ethics, then have no place within the purview of collective reason as defined by "science", so understood, and must thus be relegated to the realm of the subjective. The subject then decides, on the basis of his experiences, what he considers tenable in matters of religion, and the subjective "conscience" becomes the sole arbiter of what is ethical.

#49) In this way, though, ethics and religion lose their power to create a community and become a completely personal matter. This is a dangerous state of affairs for humanity, as we see from the disturbing pathologies of religion and reason which necessarily erupt when reason is so reduced that questions of religion and ethics no longer concern it. Attempts to construct an ethic from the rules of evolution or from psychology and sociology, end up being simply inadequate.

#50) Before I draw the conclusions to which all this has been leading, I must briefly refer to the third stage of dehellenization, which is now in progress.

#51) In the light of our experience with cultural pluralism, it is often said nowadays that the synthesis with Hellenism achieved in the early Church was an initial inculturation which ought not to be binding on other cultures. The latter are said to have the right to return to the simple message of the New Testament prior to that inculturation, in order to inculturate it anew in their own particular milieux.

#52) This thesis is not simply false, but it is coarse and

lacking in precision. The New Testament was written in Greek and bears the imprint of the Greek spirit, which had already come to maturity as the Old Testament developed.

#53) True, there are elements in the evolution of the early Church which do not have to be integrated into all cultures. Nonetheless, the fundamental decisions made about the relationship between faith and the use of human reason are part of the faith itself; they are developments consonant with the nature of faith itself.

#54) And so I come to my conclusion. This attempt, painted with broad strokes, at a critique of modern reason from within has nothing to do with putting the clock back to the time before the Enlightenment and rejecting the insights of the modern age. The positive aspects of modernity are to be acknowledged unreservedly: we are all grateful for the marvellous possibilities that it has opened up for mankind and for the progress in humanity that has been granted to us.

#55) The scientific ethos, moreover, is – as you yourself mentioned, Magnificent Rector – the will to be obedient to the truth, and, as such, it embodies an attitude which belongs to the essential decisions of the Christian spirit.

#56) The intention here is not one of retrenchment or negative criticism, but of broadening our concept of reason and its application. While we rejoice in the new possibilities open to humanity, we also see the dangers arising from these possibilities and we must ask ourselves how we can overcome them. We will succeed in doing so only if reason and faith come together in a new way, if we overcome the self-imposed limitation of reason to the empirically falsifiable, and if we once more disclose its vast horizons.

#57) In this sense theology rightly belongs in the university and within the wide-ranging dialogue of sciences, not merely as a historical discipline and one of the human sciences, but precisely as theology, as inquiry into the rationality of faith. Only thus do we become capable of that genuine dialogue of cultures and religions so urgently needed today.

#58) In the Western world it is widely held that only positivistic reason and the forms of philosophy based on it are universally valid. Yet the world's profoundly religious cultures see this exclusion of the divine from the universality of reason as an attack on their most profound convictions. A reason which is deaf to the divine and which relegates religion into the realm of subcultures is incapable of entering into the dialogue of cultures.

#59) At the same time, as I have attempted to show, modern scientific reason with its intrinsically Platonic element bears within itself a question which points beyond itself and beyond the possibilities of its methodology. Modern scientific reason quite simply has to accept the rational structure of matter and the correspondence between our spirit and the prevailing rational structures of nature as a given, on which its methodology has to be based.

#60) Yet the question why this has to be so is a real question, and one which has to be remanded by the natural sciences to other modes and planes of thought – to philosophy and theology. For philosophy and, albeit in a different way, for theology, listening to the great experiences and insights of the religious traditions of humanity, and those of the Christian faith in particular, is a source of knowledge, and to ignore it would be an unacceptable restriction of our listening and responding.

#61) Here I am reminded of something Socrates said to Phaedo. In their earlier conversations, many false philosophical opinions had been raised, and so Socrates says: "It would be easily understandable if someone became so annoyed at all these false notions that for the rest of his life he despised and mocked all talk about being – but in this way he would be deprived of the truth of existence and would suffer a great loss".[13]

#62) The West has long been endangered by this aversion to the questions which underlie its rationality, and can only suffer great harm thereby. The courage to engage the whole breadth of reason, and not the denial of its grandeur – this is the programme with which a theology grounded in Biblical faith enters into the debates of our time.

#63) "Not to act reasonably, not to act with *logos*, is contrary to the nature of God", said Manuel II, according to his Christian understanding of God, in response to his Persian interlocutor. It is to this great *logos*, to this breadth of reason, that we invite our partners in the dialogue of cultures. To rediscover it constantly is the great task of the university.

Endnotes

*   Copyright 2006 – Libreria Editrice Vaticana.
1. Of the total number of 26 conversations (διάλεξις – Khoury translates this as "controversy") in the dialogue ("Entretien"), T. Khoury published the 7th "controversy" with footnotes and an extensive introduction on the origin of the text, on the manuscript tradition and on the structure of the dialogue, together with brief summaries of the "controversies" not included in the edition; the Greek text is accompanied by a French translation: "Manuel II Paléologue, Entretiens avec un Musulman. 7ᵉ Controverse", *Sources Chrétiennes* n. 115, Paris 1966. In the meantime, Karl Förstel published in *Corpus Islamico-Christianum* (*Series Graeca* ed. A. T. Khoury and R. Glei) an edition of the text in Greek and German with commentary: "Manuel II. Palaiologus, Dialoge mit einem Muslim", 3 vols., Würzburg-Altenberge 1993–1996. As early as 1966, E. Trapp had published the Greek text with an introduction as vol. II of *Wiener byzantinische Studien*. I shall be quoting from Khoury's edition.
2. On the origin and redaction of the dialogue, cf. Khoury, pp. 22–29; extensive comments in this regard can also be found in the editions of Förstel and Trapp.
3. Controversy VII, 2 c: Khoury, pp. 142–143; Förstel, vol. I, VII. Dialog 1.5, pp. 240–241. In the Muslim world, this quotation has unfortunately been taken as an expression of my personal position, thus arousing understandable indignation. I hope that the reader of my text can see immediately that this sentence does not express my personal view of the Qur'an, for which I have the respect due to the holy book of a great religion. In quoting the text of the Emperor Manuel II, I intended solely to draw out the essential relationship between faith and reason. On this point I am in agreement with Manuel II, but without endorsing his polemic.
4. Controversy VII, 3 b–c: Khoury, pp. 144–145; Förstel vol. I, VII. Dialog 1.6, pp. 240–243.

5. It was purely for the sake of this statement that I quoted the dialogue between Manuel and his Persian interlocutor. In this statement the theme of my subsequent reflections emerges.

6. Cf. Khoury, p. 144, n. 1.

7. R. Arnaldez, *Grammaire et théologie chez Ibn Hazm de Cordoue*, Paris 1956, p. 13; cf. Khoury, p. 144. The fact that comparable positions exist in the theology of the late Middle Ages will appear later in my discourse.

8. Regarding the widely discussed interpretation of the episode of the burning bush, I refer to my book *Introduction to Christianity*, London 1969, pp. 77–93 (originally published in German as *Einführung in das Christentum*, Munich 1968; N.B. the pages quoted refer to the entire chapter entitled "The Biblical Belief in God"). I think that my statements in that book, despite later developments in the discussion, remain valid today.

9. Cf. A. Schenker, "L'Écriture sainte subsiste en plusieurs formes canoniques simultanées", in *L'Interpretazione della Bibbia nella Chiesa. Atti del Simposio promosso dalla Congregazione per la Dottrina della Fede*, Vatican City 2001, pp. 178–186.

10. On this matter I expressed myself in greater detail in my book *The Spirit of the Liturgy*, San Francisco 2000, pp. 44–50.

11. Of the vast literature on the theme of dehellenization, I would like to mention above all: A. Grillmeier, "Hellenisierung-Judaisierung des Christentums als Deuteprinzipien der Geschichte des kirchlichen Dogmas", in idem, *Mit ihm und in ihm. Christologische Forschungen und Perspektiven*, Freiburg 1975, pp. 423–488.

12. Newly published with commentary by Heino Sonnemans (ed.): *Joseph Ratzinger-Benedikt XVI, Der Gott des Glaubens und der Gott der Philosophen. Ein Beitrag zum Problem der theologia naturalis*, Johannes-Verlag Leutesdorf, 2nd revised edition, 2005.

13. Cf. 90 c–d. For this text, cf. also R. Guardini, *Der Tod des Sokrates*, 5th edition, Mainz-Paderborn 1987, pp. 218–221.

Appendix II

ON THE TERM "ISLAMO-FASCISM"

I.

The war in which we are currently engaged confuses us, in part because many will not admit it is a war. We do not know what to call it. Nor do we know what to call the self-declared enemy who has been attacking us in one form or another for some twenty-five years, ever more visibly and dangerously since 9/11-2001 with subsequent events in Afghanistan, Iraq, Spain, London, Bombay, Bali, Paris, Lebanon, and Israel. Those there are who insist that it is not a "war" at all but perhaps, at best, a police issue, no big problem. Others contend that it is a result of American or Western expansionism so that its cure is simply for us to return to our frontiers and be content with what we have. If we do this withdrawal, every threat will immediately cease at this point. No, in another view, it is due to poverty and oppression, even though most of the perpetrators of the war are quite rich. Yet another interpretation is that this turmoil stems from a very small minority with no relation to national or religious origins, a kind of floating international brigade of bandits, like the Mafia, out for their own profit and glory. The variants on these themes are almost infinite.

What names should we use that will accurately define and designate the cause? Calling things by their right names is the first requirement of reality; refusing to do so, the first cause of confusion, if not defeat. At first, we were told that the war is against something called "terrorism." Its perpetrators were logically called "terrorists." It was considered "hate-language" to call them anything else. However, we find listed on no map a place called "Terroritoria," where said "terrorists" otherwise dwell in peace plotting our demise. It has no capital, no military uniform for its mostly invisible troops, no rules of combat. In this designation, some difficulty ensues when we try to identify or designate a group that just wants to "terrorize" others, as if that is an explanation. Some may like to travel or to fish for pleasure; they like "terror" for terror's sake, just a question of taste.

Of course, this membership in a supposed organization called "Terror International" is not what the known "terrorists" claim for themselves. They look on this designation with contempt since it misses the whole nature of what they think that they are doing. But the term "terrorism" seems temporarily useful because it avoids the politics of naming more carefully just who these actual men (and women) are who carry out these, to us, seemingly senseless bombings. Are they so "senseless" after all? That is, do they have their own rationale and are we intellectually willing to face what it is?

All along, as a chief tactic of the "terrorists," we have had "suicide bombers." "Suicide bombing" is, thus far, the main delivery system of the "terrorists." It is remarkably effective in creating immediate chaos. We have almost forgotten how used we have become to this utterly corrupt practice that undermines, and seeks to undermine, the very basis of any possible civilization opposed to it. Those who practice "suicide bombing" (it is a once-in-a-lifetime occupation, to be sure) called themselves "martyrs." They are, when successful, treated as heroes by other "terrorists" and their admirers. Thus, the same action is called in one political zone "terrorism," while, in another, it is called "martyrdom." What do words mean?

To perform this switch of meaning, of course, the "terrorists" had also to call the "victims" of "suicide bombers," not innocent objects of terrorism, as we call them, but guilty opponents of the cause for which "terrorism" really stands, its religious mission in the world. Even when people of one's own religion are killed, they are said, theologically, like the "suicide bombers" themselves, to have been done a favor in reaching heaven more quickly.

So what language do we use to speak of this horrendous situation? We also hear used the word "Islamicist," or "Islamism." We hear "Jihadists," or holy warriors. We are struck with the fierceness with which the "terrorists" themselves reject being called "fascists" or, what they also are, "terrorists." They sense that the term, "Islamo-fascism," or any of its variants, undermines or disparages, what, in their own minds, is the legitimacy or morality of their "cause." We have here an issue that forces us to consider the very roots of the "terrorists'" understanding of their own motivations.

The fact that almost all the "terrorists," no matter their country of birth, have Muslim origins, moreover, brings us up against our own ecumenical or liberal theories which do not allow us to "profile" or stigmatize or even accuse of bad motives those who do carry out the killings. The argument goes: All religions are "peaceful." Islam is a religion. Therefore, Islam is peaceful. This is not a historical syllogism that explains the actual record of the expansion of Islam from its beginning in Arabia till its reaching Tours in the eighth century and Vienna in the sixteenth. Nor does it explain the violence and law used within Muslim states to prevent any expression of faith or philosophy that does not conform to their own understanding of the Koran. This earlier expansion was almost exclusively by military conquest, often extremely brutal, against Christian, Persian, Hindu, or other lands.

II.

More recently, the term "Islamo-fascism" has been coined in an effort to describe the source and nature of "terrorism." I want to examine the appropriateness of this term, as I think it serves to get at the core of the problem. Is "Islamo-fascism" really accurate for what the reality is? Initially, the term obviously is not a product of Islamic thinkers thinking of themselves, though some more recent Muslim thinkers have studied the Marxists and the fascists. No Imam in Iran or Egypt, however, suddenly wakes up in the middle of the night and shouts, "That's it! I am an Islamo-fascist; why did I not think of that before?" No pious youth in Mecca reads the Collected Works of Benito Mussolini and muses to himself, "Yes, this is what Mohammed was about in the Koran."

Rather the term comes from Western politicians and writers. They are desperately seeking a word or expression that they can use, one that avoids suggesting that the war in fact has religious roots, as the people who are doing the attacking claim it does. To say that war has "religious" roots violates a code, a constitutional principle. Wars are political, not religious. Therefore, their explanation must be political, must arise from modern political science. Hobbes, "where are you when we need you?" Religion cannot be a serious motivation, especially over the centuries. We must look elsewhere. Only social "science" can explain this phenomenon.

"Fascism," in this context, thus becomes a handy term. We thought that we were rid of that menace after World War II, of course. Compared to Marxism and Nazism, it was, in fact, the mildest of the ideologies of our recent time. Many of its features, originally designed for other situations, can appear to apply to what is going on in our "terrorist"-infected world. This happy analytic result, it is said, justifies us in joining "Islam" and "fascism" together in a way that apparently absolves most of Islam of anything to do with the problem or any responsibility for themselves doing anything about it. At the same time, it demonstrates the usefulness of Western political science in understanding modern movements. If science cannot understand something, it cannot be understood, as it were.

If for no other reason than the sake of clarity, let us think our way further through this murky issue of what to call what we are dealing with. We have to call it something because it is something. It will not "go away" peacefully any time soon. Aristotle indicated that the first issue in political things is to describe accurately the nature of a regime under scrutiny. What exactly is it? This seemingly simple explanatory effort can itself be quite dangerous, quite personally dangerous, as Muslims who question their own roots soon find out. Many powerful, even many weak, governments do not like to be called what they scientifically are. Moreover, a distinction can be found between what some political thing is and what we are allowed to call it because of our own philosophical or political positions. The political control of language, as George Orwell suggested, is itself an instrument of tyranny. Moreover, such a thing as political philosophy exists even apart from any actual regime and what it allows us to call it.

We should by now be used to totalitarian regimes insisting on calling themselves "republics" or "democracies" and punishing anyone who refuses to accept a government's own definition of itself. Today, the accurate use of language, apparently something guaranteed in our amendments, is a minefield. We have something like "hate crimes" whose effect is in fact to prevent us from naming exactly what we are dealing with. Philosophy in these circumstances is driven underground. The phenomenon of philosophy being driven underground was, as Leo Strauss once remarked, a major issue within medieval Islamic philosophy.

III.

The Washington Times recently (August 12, 2006) published a useful and insightful editorial, "It's Fascism," that I will use to comment on this nomenclature. First, the editorial points out the gradual change in President Bush's designation of the enemy. He, with Mr. Blair, began using the word "terrorist," but more recently he has used the designation "fascist." "Is this a legitimate use?" the editorial asks itself. Fascism, it continues, is a "political philosophy" that exalts a group or nation over the individual. It could also imply a religion. Fascism promoted central rule, subordinated individuals to "political leadership." The term thus can legitimately be used to designate those responsible for the recent "terrorist" understandings of themselves.

The editorial identifies groups like "al Qaeda, Hezbollah, Hamas" and other organizations as "fascist," that is, they operate in effect on these principles. "Non-Muslims" are regarded as "a lesser breed of expendable or contemptible dhimmis and infidels." Social and economic restrictions are placed on every group that does not conform to the ruling power. The editorial says that "this is not mainstream Islam. . . . It is a corruption of the faith."

Evidently, *The Washington Times* was among the first to use this designation "Islamofascism." It was related to a German-born Muslim scholar, Kalid Duran, in an interview about his book, *An Introduction to Islam for Jews*, in *The Washington Times*. In spite of Muslim organization protests, the editorial maintained that its use of the term was simply an accurate description of what, with proper distinctions, these people did. "Islamofascism speaks for itself. It is a real phenomenon." It is not illegal, immoral, or even impolite to call it what, judging from its actions, it is.

The question I ask, in the light of this case for the use of the term "Islamofascism," is this: does this term clarify or obscure the issue? Let me propose a thought process. Recently, a friend told me of reading a report from London that one of the "terrorists" designated to blow up a transatlantic flight planned to be accompanied by his wife and child. The explosive was to be in the baby's bottle. The man was willing thus to blow up himself, his wife, and child in the cause for which these ten or so planes were to be destroyed by similar methods.

Now this proposal, in itself, strikes any of us as simply horrendous, insane, mad. Moreover, let us suppose that the plot was not detected and was successful. Within the course of several hours, analogous to the relative success of 9/11, ten planes with a total of, say, two or three thousand passengers flying from London to New York had been destroyed. What would the reaction of this news have been in Tehran or Cairo or other Muslim capitals? I would like to be wrong on this, but judging from previous instances, I greatly fear that, in too many cases, there would have been cheering, not horror. This heinous act would have been interpreted, not by all but by many, as a stunning success and a blow at the great Satan. We would probably have heard from the President of Iran or Osama bin Laden himself or someone of that level that more was in store, that the final day of reckoning is nearer.

What do these speculations have to do with the term "Islamofascism?" When 9/11 first happened, I recall commenting on this very issue, this time in the case of the young men who plotted, planned, and carried out the destruction of the World Trade Center. What, in their own minds, did they think they were doing? Did they think they were executing an "Islamofascist" plot? Hardly. Did they think they were in it for money? Surely not. They were in it for the glory that comes from what they saw to be the "brave" act of destroying the symbol of the great enemy, his communication center. This act would go down in sacred history as the first step. Other successes would surely follow.

What was in it for themselves? Exactly what their religion said was in it. They were doing the work of Allah. The world could not know peace until it was subjugated to his rule as laid down in the holy book. The advance had been stymied for hundreds of years, set back, but now a new, glorious opportunity arose. Young men, willing to die, flocked to the cause. There is a sense of purpose, the reestablishment of the Caliphate, the subjugation and elimination of the enemies, the Christians, the Jews, the

Hindus, the Chinese. Not all would be eliminated, of course. It is a religion of peace. All would be "converted," except perhaps for a few insignificant ones. This is why Islam is in the world.

But, one might protest, are there no rules about means? And Islam is said to want to achieve these world goals "peacefully." My only point in following this question of the use of the word "Islamofascism" is that it does not describe what these men think they are doing. Nor does it help that some thus far ineffective Muslim apologists do not think that the term describes what the religion means. It is what these men think and evidently practice. What has to take place, in response, is some more adequate confrontation with the incoherence of this claim to world-subjection to Allah as an inner-worldly political mission powered by a quasi-mystical devotion to its cause. In this sense, in the minds of the ones carrying out the attacks, it is religious, not ideological, in origin.

A somewhat bewildered American President and British Prime Minister have understood, whereas many politicians have not, that there is a real war and a real enemy. They have been prudent in their use of language, catering to differing usages both in Western democracies and in the Muslim world. Their general approach has been to seek to isolate the "terrorists" from the rest of the Muslim world. This world itself has been caught up for centuries in a stagnant and almost totally controlled system, usually under the power of a military that has served to sit on top of those religious radicals who would tear up the world. What the President thus has sought to do is finally to allow and encourage what he considers to be the great majority of Muslim citizens to be able to participate in a culture that is not dominated by such motives that burst forth frequently from within Islam to employ terror.

Just as *The Washington Times* proposes "Islamofascism" to describe what these missionary groups do to further their cause, so the President proposes "democracy" as the alternative way of life that would both mitigate the fanaticism and allow the majority to escape into their own self-ruling states. One drawback of this solution is often the internal moral condition of the democracies themselves. The "terrorists" never tire of pointing to this inner corruption that often manifests itself within our own souls. So there is a kind of war on two fronts that comes forth from thinking about "Islamofascism," that envisioned by the "terrorists" themselves and that of the alternative they see in us which justifies, in their own minds, their violent ways.

Words, I am sure, have to be themselves used "wisely." It is not always easy to describe or hear what we actually are. The root cause of "suicide bombers" and the attacks of the "terrorists" are not primarily in Western political philosophy. The "suicide bombers," in effect, while they sometimes learn to use sophisticated weapons, have shown the folly of much discussion about nuclear weapons – the weapons are not the problem, but who has them. Moreover, as 9/11 showed, modern civilization is so complex that even the simplest acts like flying a plane into a building are as lethal as anything we can conceive. No one doubts, however, that these "terrorists" would use more sophisticated means if they could manage it.

In the meantime, one or two potential terrorists have made every one of us take our shoes off or empty our bottles before we fly anywhere in the world. The cost of their even trying unsuccessfully to blow us up is itself astronomical. The first question remains, not "how do we protect themselves from their threats?" We must ask that too. But the first question has to be, "why in the first place do they still want to threaten and, yes, conquer us?" I suspect we cannot answer this latter question primarily for reasons within our own political philosophy.

Originally published as "On the Meaning of the Term "Islamo-Fascism" in *Ignatius Insight* (August 15, 2006). Used with permission.

BIBLIOGRAPHY

Books

Adam, Karl, *The Son of Man* (Garden City, N.Y.: Doubleday Image, [1934] 1960).

Ali, Daniel and Robert Spencer, *Inside Islam: A Guide for Catholics: 100 Questions and Answers* (West Chester, Pa.: Ascension Press, 2003).

Arkes, Hadley, *First Things: An Inquiry into the First Principles of Morals and Justice* (Princeton, N.J.: Princeton University Press, 1986).

Aslan, Reza, *No God but God: The Origins, Evolution, and Future of Islam* (New York: Random House, 2006).

Averröes on Plato's "Republic," translated by Ralph Lerner (Ithaca, N.Y.: Cornell University Press, 1974).

Belloc, Hilaire, *The Crusade: The World's Debate* (London: Cassell, 1937).

———, *The Great Heresies* (New York: Sheed & Ward, 1938).

Bochenski, J. M., *Philosophy – an Introduction*, (New York: Harper Colophon, 1972).

Budziszewski, J., *Natural Law for Lawyers* (Nashville: ACW Press, 2006).

Charles, J. Daryl, *Between Pacifism and Jihad: Just War and Christian Tradition* (Downers Grove, Ill.: Inter-Varsity, 2005).

Cocker, H. H., *Triumph* (Roseville, Cal.: Forum, 2001).

Cooper, Barry, *New Political Religions, or an Analysis of Modern Terrorism* (Columbia: University of Missouri Press, 2004).

Copleston, Frederick, *Medieval Philosophy* (New York: Harper Torchbooks, 1961).

Daniélou, Jean, *La crise actuelle de l'intelligence* (Paris: Apostolat des Editions, 1969).

Dawson, Christopher, *The Making of Europe* (New York: Meridian, 1956).

———, *Medieval Essays* (Garden City, N.Y.: Doubleday Image, 1959.

———, *Religion and Culture* (New York: Meridian, 1962).

———. *Religion and the Rise of Western Culture* (Garden City, N.Y.: Doubleday Image, 1958).

Deane, Herbert, *Political and Social Ideas of St. Augustine* (New York: Columbia University Press, 1956).

De Lubac, Henri, *A Brief Catecchesis on Nature & Grace* (San Francisco: Ignatius, 1984).

———, *Catholicism: Christ and the Common Destiny of Man* (San Francisco: Ignatius, [1947] 1988).

De Wulf, Maurice, *Philosophy & Civilization in the Middle Ages* (New York: Dover, 1950).

Elsthain, Jean Bethke, *Augustine and the Limits of Politics* (Notre Dame, Ind.: University of Notre Dame Press, 1995).

Esposito, John, *Unholy War: Terror in the Name of Islam* (New York: Oxford, 2002).

Gilson, Etienne, *God and Philosophy* (New Haven, Conn.: Yale University Press, 1941).

———, *History of Christian Philosophy in the Middle Ages* (New York: Random House, 1955).

———, *Reason and Revelation in the Middle Ages* (New York: Scribner's, 1938).

———, *The Unity of Philosophical Experience* (San Francisco: Ignatius [1938] 1999).

Glorious Koran, text and explanatory translation by Muhaammad Pickthall (Elmhurst, N.Y.: Tahrike Tarsile Qur'an, 1999).

Heidegger, Martin, *What Is Philosophy?* Translated by J. Wilde and W Klubach (New Haven, Conn.: College & University Press, 1956).

Jaki, Stanley, L., *The Road of Science and the Ways to God* (Chicago: University of Chicago Press, 1979).

———, *Jesus, Islam, Science* (Port Huron, Mich.: Real Value Books, 2001).

Bibliography

Jomier, Jacques, *The Bible and the Qur'an* (San Francisco: Ignatius, [1959] 2002).

Kass, Leon, *The Beginning of Wisdom* (New York: The Free Press, 2003).

————, *The Hungry Soul: Eating and the Perfecting of Our Nature* (New York: The Free Press, 1994).

Kreeft, Peter, *The Philosophy of Jesus* (South Bend, Ind.: St. Augustine's Press, 2007).

Ledeen, Michael, *The War against the Terror Masters* (New York: St. Martin's Press, 2002).

The Legacy of Jihad: Islamic Holy War and the Fate of Non-Muslims, edited by Andrew C. Bostom (Amherst, N.Y.: Prometheus Books, 2005).

Lewis, C. S., *The Abolition of Man* (New York: Macmillan, 1947).

MacIntyre, Alasdair, *After Virtue: A Study of Moral Theory* (Notre Dame, Ind.: University of Notre Dame Press, 1983).

Manent, Pierre, *The City of Man* (Princeton, N.J.: Princeton University Press, 1998).

McCoy, Charles N. R., *The Structure of Political Thought* (New York: McGraw-Hill, 1963).

Medieval Political Philosophy, edited by Ralph Lerner and Muhsin Mahdi (Ithaca, N.Y.: Cornell University Press, 1963).

Medieval Political Thought: c. 350–c. 1450, edited by J. H. Burns (The Cambridge History; New York: Cambridge University Press, 1991).

Murawiec, Laurent, *The Mind of Jihad* (Washington: The Hudson Institute, 2005).

Muslims and the West: Encounter and Dialogue, edited by Zafar Ishaq Ansari and John Esposito (Washington: Georgetown University, 2002).

O'Donovan, Oliver, and Joan Lockwood O'Donovan, editors, *From Irenaeus to Grotius: A Sourcebook in Christian Political Thought* (Grand Rapids, Mich.: Eerdmans, 1999).

Qutb, Sayyid, *Milestones* (Indianapolis: American Trust Publications, 1990).

Owens, Joseph, *Human Destiny: Some Problems for Catholic Philosophy* (Washington, D.C.: Catholic University of America Press, 1985).

Pangle, Thomas, *Political Philosophy and the God of Abraham* (Baltimore: The Johns Hopkins University Press, 2005).

Pernoud, Régine, *Those Terrible Middle Ages* (San Francisco: Ignatius, 2000).

Phares, Walid, *Future Jihad: Terrorist Strategies against America.*

Pickstock, Catherine, *After Writing: On the Liturgical Consummation of Philosophy* (Oxford: Blackwell, 1998).

Pieper, Josef, *In Defence of Philosophy* (San Francisco: Ignatius, 1992).

————, *Guide to Thomas Aquinas* (San Francisco: Ignatius, 1991).

————, *Scholasticism: Personalities and Problems of Medieval Philosophy* (New York: McGraw-Hill, 1960; St. Augustine's Press, 2001).

Rahner, Hugo, *Church and State in Early Christianity* (San Francisco: Ignatius, 1992).

Rasmussen, Martha, *The Catholic Church: The First 2000 Years* (San Francisco: Ignatius, 2003).

Ratzinger, Joseph, (Pope Benedict XVI), *God Is Love (Deus Caritas Est)* (San Francisco: Ignatius, 2006).

————, *Introduction to Christianity* (New York: Herder and Herder, 1969).

————, *Milestones: Memoirs 1927–1977* (San Francisco: Ignatius, 1998).

————, *Salt of the Earth: The Church at the End of the Millennium: An Interview with Peter Seewald* (San Francisco: Ignatius, 1997).

————, *The Spirit of the Liturgy* (San Francisco: Ignatius, 2000).

————, *Turning Point for Europe?* (San Francisco: Ignatius, 1994).

Rowland, Tracey, *Culture and the Thomist Tradition* (London: Routledge, 2003).

Royal, Robert, *The Catholic Martyrs of the Twentieth Century: A Comprehensive World History* (New York: Crossroad, 2000).

Schall, James V, *At the Limits of Political Philosophy* (Washington, D.C.: The Catholic University of America Press, 1996).

————, *The Life of the Mind: The Joys and Travails of Thinking* (Wilmington, Del.: ISI Books, 2006).

————, *Reason, Revelation, and the Foundations of Political Philosophy* (Baton Rouge: Louisiana State University Press, 1987).

————, *Roman Catholic Political Philosophy* (Lanham, Md.: Lexington Books, 2004).

Schumacher, E. F., *A Guide for the Perplexed* (New York: Harper Colophon, 1977).

Scruton, Roger, *The West and the Rest: Globalization and the Terrorist Threat* (Wilmington, Del.: ISI Books, 2002).

Sokolowski, Robert, *Christian Faith & Human Understanding* (Washington, D.C.: Catholic University of America Press, 2005).

————, *The God of Faith and Reason* (Washington, D.C.: Catholic University of America Press, 1996).

Solzhenitsyn, Alexander, *Solzhenitsyn at Harvard*, edited by R. Berman (Washington, D.C.: Ethics and Public Policy, 1980).

Spenser, Robert, *The Truth about Muhammed* (Washington: Regnery, 2006).

Strauss, Leo, *Persecution and the Art of Writing* (Westport, Conn.: Greenwood Press, 1973).

————, *Rebirth of Classical Political Rationalism*, edited by Thomas Pangle (Chicago: University of Chicago Press, 1989).

————, *Studies in Platonic Political Philosophy* (Chicago: University of Chicago Press, 1983).

————, *What Is Political Philosophy? And Other Essays* (Glencoe, Ill.: The Free Press, 1959).

Voegelin, Eric, *New Science of Politics* (Chicago: University of Chicago Press, 1952).

Von Hildebrand, Dietrich, *What Is Philosophy?* (New York: Routledge, 1960).

Wallace, William, *The Modeling of Nature: Philosophy of Science and Philosophy of Nature in Synthesis* (Washington, D.C.: The Catholic University of America Press, 1996).

Wilhelmsen, Frederick, *The Paradoxical Structure of Existence* (Albany, N.Y.: Preserving Christian Publications, 1995).

Ye'or, Bat, *Eurabia: The Euro-Arab Axis* (Madison, N.J.: Fairleigh Dickenson University Press, 2005).

Periodical Essays

"After van Gogh: Islamic Terrorism in Europe," *The Economist*, London, November 14, 2004.

Bar, Shmuel, "The Religious Sources of Islamic Terrorism," *Policy Review*, 2005, #125. prlogosm.gif

BenDedek, R. P., "Wafa Sultan – Some Muslims Do Speak Out"; http://magic-city-news.com/article_5476.shtml

Browne, Anthony, "The Triumph of the East." www.uriasposten/de/kopier/Spectator-240704–Browne-TriumphEast.htm

Bynum, Rebecca, "Freedom: True and False," *New English Review*, October, 2006.

Carey, Lord George, "The Cross and the Crescent: The Clash of Faiths in an Age of Secularism," The Beach Lecture, Newbold College, Brecknell, September 18, 2006.

Fernandez-Morera, Dario, "The Myth of the Andalusian Paradise," *The Intercollegiate Review*, 41 (Fall, 3006), 23–31.

Gabriel, Brigitte, "Real Intelligence on Islamic Violence," *The Herald Examiner*, 20 (October, 2006), 1, 3.

Harris, Lee, "Socrates or Muhammad? Joseph Ratzinger on the Destiny of Reason," *The Weekley Standard*, 12 (#3, 2006).

Ibrahim, Youssef, "America and Islam: Collision Inevitable?" *The New York Sun*, June 19, 2006.

"In the Name of Islam," *The Economist*, London, Survey, September 13, 2003, 14 pp.

Magister, Sandro, "Islamist Terrorism: What the Vatican Really Thinks," www.chiesa. October 6, 2004.

Muqtedar Khan, M. A., "Muslims Must Develop an Intolerance for Intolerance." www.ijtihad.org/intolerance.htm.

Nayed, Aref Ali, "The Image of a Violent, Un-reasonable Islam," www.chiesa. September, 2006

"Open Letter to His Holiness Pope Benedict XVI," 36 Muslim Scholars, 2006.

Phares, Walid, "A Patient Enemy," Silwa News, Sept. 28, 2006, 5 pp.

"The Pope and the Prophet," *The London Times*, Editorial, September 16, 2006.

Reilly, Robert, "The Pope and the Prophet," *Crisis*, 24 (November, 2006), 18–23.

————, *The Roots of Islamist Ideology*, CPCE Briefing Paper, London: Center for Research into Post-Communist Economies, February, 2006. 13 pp.

Samir Khalil Samir, S.J., "For a Definitive Peace Settlement in the Middle East," http://www.chiesa.espressoonline.it/dettaglio. jsp?d-80221&eng=y

Samuelson, Robert, "Collapsing Birthrates in Industrialized Countries," *Washington Post*, May 24, 2006.

Schall, James V., "A Brief War Primer," *The Best Catholic Writing, 2005*, edited by B. Doyle (Chicago: Loyola Press, 2005), 113–20.

————, "Islam Will Not Be the Loser," *Dossier*, 8 (January/February, 2002), 8–14.

————, "Ratzinger on Europe," *Homiletic and Pastoral Review*, CV (January, 2005), 41–45.

————, "Ratzinger on the Modern Mind," *Homiletic and Pastoral Review*, XCVIII (October, 1997), 6–14.

————, "When Wars Must Be the Answer," *Policy Review*, #128, December, 2004, January, 2005, 59–70.

Schwartz, Robert, "Radical Islam in America," *Imprimis*, 33 (May, 2004), 1–7.

Scruton, Roger, "'Islamofascism': Beware of a Religion without Irony," *The Wall Street Journal*, August 20, 2006; www.opinion-journal.com/editorial/feature. html?id=110008822

Spaemann, Robert, "Rationality and Faith in God," *Communio*, 32 (Winter, 2005).

Steyn, Mark, "Births 'n Dearths: Deadly Demography," *National Review*, October 23, 2006, 44–46.

"Suicide Bombers Follow Quran," *WorldNetDaily*, September 27, 2006; http://www.worldnetdaily.com/news/article.asp?ARTI-CLE_ID=521d84

Thomas, Cal, "Moderate, Peaceful Islam: Where Is the Evidence?" September 10, 2004. www.NewsAnd Opinion.com

Trifkovic, Serge, "Understanding the Terrorists' Mindset," www.chroniclemagazine.org/cgi-bin/newsview.cg

Varadarajan, Tunka, "Prophet of Decline: An Interview with Oriana Fallaci," *The Wall Street Journal*, June 23, 2005.

Warren, David, "Thanks to the Pope, Now We're Talking," *Ottawa Citizen*, October 24, 2006.

Ye'or, Bat, "Hearing on Religious Persecution in the Middle East," Senate Foreign Relations Committee, *Congressional Record*, May 1, 1997; (http://mypage.bluewin.ch/ameland/LectureE3.html).

INDEX